WRITING DIRTY WORDS

the not-so-sexy hustle of making a living writing— and the occasional crack of the whip

BY RALPH GRECO, JR.

Writing Dirty Words
Copyright 2023 by Ralph Greco, Jr.
ISBN 978-1-957863-14-6 Paperback
ISBN 978-1-957863-15-3 ebook

Published by Parisian Phoenix Publishing, Easton, Pennsylvania USA

Design Credits
Cover Photo: STILLFX, istockphoto.com

C O N N E C T with the publisher:
◎ Parisian Phoenix
◐ ParisBirdBooks
✉ angel@parisianphoenix.com

C O N N E C T with the author:
✉ ralphiedawriter@gmail.com

TABLE OF CONTENTS

INTRODUCTION

"The erotic romance genre brings in over a billion dollars annually, and Amazon reports sales of approximately $9.7 million a year in erotic eBooks. So, while it may be cliché to say sex sells, the stats show that authors can make a good income from penning porn," said my good friend, "Domina Doll," fellow naughty writer and marketer. Domina offered this tidbit for a press release when I began writing my *Writing Dirty Words* column at www.sexpert.com. As the then editor at this site replete with sex-positive articles, and the person who had brought me on board, I was thrilled, and agreed (and still do) whole-heartedly with Domina's comment.

It's also a great first salvo-across-the-bow for this book.

I have been writing naughty words ever since the mid 1980s when I accompanied a friend to the home of a couple running a pre-recorded #800 sex phone line. This was in the nascent days of computers, pre-cell phones, (No cell phones? Say it isn't so, Ralph!), and the couple's set-up, while wildly inventive and state-of-the-art to us then, would seem like the proverbial stone knives and bear-skin rugs these days. My friend had read an ad in a local arts paper that this guy and girl were looking for voice actresses to read and record short naughty scripts. Having no idea if the pair was legitimate, or even actually a couple and not just some creep looking to lure unsuspecting, young women to his home, my friend had me tag along. Fortunately, the couple, whose apartment was a mere ten minutes from where I lived at the time, was perfectly wonderful, safe, and sane mid-30-somethings (my friend and I were in our mid-twenties at the time). They even asked me to read a script or two, dutifully paying my friend and me for what amounted to a fun Saturday night of fake moaning, slapping our thighs to make spanking sounds and lots of giggling over Cheetos and Cokes.

Yes, we were wild partiers back then.

At the end of the evening, I happened to mention, as more an afterthought really, that if the couple ever needed someone to write some naughty little scenarios, 'scripts' they called them, I was available. Not that I had ever tried my hand at erotica. I was a stone cold supremely devoted sci-fi geek, at the time, in both what I read and what I was trying to write, and when not penning speculative short stories, I wrote songs. But I figured, why not give something naughty a try?

The husband jumped at the chance to have another writer on the team, burnt-out as he claimed he was trying to come up with naughty two-pages of dialogue and quick set-ups; although a whizz on computers and a budding entrepreneur, he admitted he wasn't a writer.

A week later, I delivered two scripts, and received my first payment for something I wrote.

My naughty writing career had begun.

If you Google my name, you will find my credits, such as they are, as much in the adult writing field as mainstream. In fact, you'll find more of me popping up in the adult field as lots of the writing I do for mainstream clients is stuff for which I am not credited or receive a byline. I won't bore you with my naughty resume, but since that script writing job just about four decades ago (ok, somebody want to tell me where the time went?) I've become a professional writer, and have continued into my professional music making, and for guts, fame, and glory, I presently make my meager daily bread from writing and playing. With my writing, which is what this books is about afterall, I seem to have as much talent (or am merely kidding myself that I do) for penning erotica, adult toy reviews, scene scripts, and porn press releases as I do for writing HVAC cleaning company website SEO copy, ghostwriting books for executives, authoring a series of children's books, writing a bunch of one-acts plays I have seen produced across America, and reviewing vintage rock music, as well as theatre and film (and a whole lot more). Like most people I meet, I have a varied set of interests, some that lead me here and there, sometimes where I least expect to find myself, but always pretty much set on an adventure at best, and an education, at least.

One of those places I found myself was giving classes at kink conventions with my good friend and great erotic fantasist writer, M. Christian.

"Chris" as he is known to his friends, which is what most people who meet the guy quickly become, is someone I not only befriended quickly, but I consider my mentor as well as one of my closest buddies. He's also my podcast co host and you can find him (and I suggest you do go out looking for him) at www.mchristian.com. Pre that wacky VID thing, 'Chris' and I traveled to St. Louis, Las Vegas, San Francisco, and New Jersey (granted for the N.J. gigs I didn't have to travel far), helming our hour-and-a-half weekend classes. We presented impactful (in more ways than one) lecture/demonstrations like "Clothespins: The Kinky Wondertoy" and "Tit-Play 101: A Breast Play Workshop." Among our offerings was also our "Writing Smut 101." This last class led me to sexpert.com, penning my bi-monthly column about dirty writing born from lessons I learned in my classes, which in turn led me to tweak some of those columns, and in many more cases, write a bunch of new ones to make this book.

In the face of comely young lasses baring breast or booty for class demonstrations (it's funny how two hetero guys like Chris and me, always seek out ripe and willing young women as our "demo subs"… go figure) our writing class was always our favorite.

Why? From the very first time Chris and got up in front of a bunch of writers, I realized how much we actually knew about writing dirty words, and how great it was that what we knew actually meant something to somebody other than ourselves. Rapid firing answers back to questions put to us, we found ourselves oh-so-thrilled over how our class attendees stayed for the full hour-and-a-half (the time really did fly by) and I dare say we learned so much more listening to our fellow writers sharing their stories than I am sure they ever got from us. And with more people approaching Chris and I at the end of each writing class than at any other class we held, we always left those writing summits bouncing on a true and unprecedented high after jawing with our fellow scribes.

As Mick and the boys termed it so long ago, these classes were indeed a "gas gas gas."

I think because what we writers do, we mostly do by ourselves, it's thrilling to share war stories, in a word, commiserate with someone else who does this voodoo that we do. I say it all the time, my buddy Chris knows about my life in a way nobody else ever will as he works through the very same daily triumphs and failures that I do. It's no different than professional chefs sharing kitchen dramas or one mechanic getting into a good long conversation with a fellow mechanic over a funny garage anecdote.

So, the writing life? The dirty word writing life specifically? Well, it's interesting, I can tell you that. There's never a dull moment (ok, there are some), and I have met some fantastic folks from doing this professionally full-time for the past 15+ years. Afforded some amazing opportunities, given not a small amount of swag ('he with the most toys at the end of the day wins,' and all that) and building my skills to a sure better degree than when I first started, I have the distinct feeling my life and career would not have gotten to this point had I stuck to writing just vanilla stuff.

Not that there is anything wrong with writing vanilla stuff, as there is nothing wrong with just writing erotica. But I feel I am more suited for and therefore grew better at writing by scribbling the niche-satirical-cross-genre-erotica that I write alongside everything else. And even though this book is bent to dirty word writing, I believe there might be some insights here or at least enough little anecdotes that will ring true for any writer. And maybe, some of what I have imparted might just speak to the creative spirit in everybody, as I do believe everybody has a creative spirit, not just writers.

Now, I am fully aware that the climate we currently live in gives many of us pause airing our opinion. I'm sorry for this. It is truly a scourge of our age that we are so scrutinized that one person's opinion simply can't be deemed simply their opinion and left at that. But this is what this book is made of…my opinions. Surely, you could look at some of the chapters below as writing 'lessons,' although I'd use the word 'lessons' very loosely. But what follows is still pretty much just my takeaways from the writing life, as much my view on the nuts-and-bolts stuff, as my take on the social part of what I do.

So, agree, disagree, write me nasty criticisms, or laud me with your compliments (I also accept PayPal bribes), but please realize that if you come across something you vehemently disagree with, well, so be it.

h

Sorry, but I'm not about to apologize.

Sure, I'd rather we get along, that you find everything I have written here to be sage advice you come to apply to an ever-more successful writing life, but I doubt this will be the case. And if I say something along the way that rankles you, be it about writing or life in general — as this writing thing I do *is* pretty much my life in general — well, put it down as just my opinion, which I hope, even in 2023, we are all still entitled to.

As I write at the beginning of all of my books, I sincerely thank you for taking the time to read me and wish you and yours the very best of health and happiness.

Ralph Greco, Jr.
ralphiedawriter@gmail.com

1.

Just Write It Already

I love Christopher Hitchens' flip witticism on the famous quote about writing.

"Everyone has a book in them and that, in most cases, is where it should stay," he said.

It's a cynical assessment clearly, and while I'm a fan of Hitchens, and this quote gives me a giggle, I don't agree. It shouldn't stay there.

I tell people all the time — students in my writing classes or friends asking for writing advice — write it. Go ahead. Who cares what it is, where it comes from, and even what it might be. It's my matter-of-fact response to that, "Hey Ralph, how does one start writing?" question to which I always reply: "Um, one just starts writing."

When Forrest Gump is asked why he started running, he says, "I just felt like runnin'." Well, most people I know who wanted to write began to do so because they just felt like....writing. My buddy Bob is fond of saying, "Writers write," and that's all there is to it. And as with all things, in order to do something, you have to take the first step and start doing it.

If you have something itching inside your noggin that you feel needs to be put down on paper, across a word document, or a missive that you just need to email to yourself, go ahead and get it out. This unadulterated yawping is especially important when it comes to naughty writing, what this book is mainly about, and the kind of scribbling from which I make a good amount of my daily bread and butter. Naughty scenes, snippets of hot dialogue, toy descriptions, interviews with porn stars and gooey description of some dangerous canoodling all come screaming out of my brain at all hours of the day, whether I am commissioned to get them out or not. And I wouldn't be where I am presently, wherever the hell that is, without slapping these words down.

From the #800 number script writing that launched me into the business, I sold a few stories to "Penthouse Letters," as well as acquired a bunch of rejections and placed one or two naughty interviews in an underground magazine. Then a buddy of mine began a copywriting service where we suddenly found lots of work with adult companies. By the time we slipped officially into 'the biz' in 2009, the Internet and erotica/adult marketing were exploding, so my partner and I made the best of it.

We wrote ad copy, blogs, product descriptions, articles, and newsletter updates, to name just a smidgen of what we go into. Whatever a client needed, my friend and I would provide. I managed the bulk of the writing, while my partner applied her acumen to the actual marketing and placement of my words, and we both courted the clients, whether together, or through our personal contacts. From there, I haven't looked back (ok, maybe when the collection agencies are at the door), inching my way forward each day through my writing, enjoying the wonderful people I continue to meet, and just by keeping my eyes and ears open, best I can when I damn well am fighting the urge for nappies come 3:30 or so.

Beyond your inner scolding of, 'I can't write this stuff down, what if somebody sees?' and the 'I don't even want to be thinking about this, let alone writing it!' there will come plenty of other obstacles to keep you from writing dirty words, or keep you from writing in general. I encounter them even now, from mainstream clients who balk when they hear about the 'other' kind of writing I do to even the voice in my head that says to me, 'You know Ralph, you are probably the only person in the world who wants to read about robot copulation on Mars.'

I've found that, no, I'm not the only one.

Certainly, naughty word writing is not for everyone to try or for everyone to read. But I genuinely believe that have you a craving to make words that describe an encounter between the "beast of two backs" or any other beast, let it fly. Don't stop yourself before you even begin. Actually, this let-it-out philosophy will serve you for really anything you have a burning desire to do. Do it, make it, render it, fire it, sculpt it, paint it, plant it. Just get the thing out of you.

There really is no other way to do it then just to do it!

So, what are you doing there, reading? Get off your ass and start writing!

2.

Erotica Or Porn: That Is The Question...
Or Is It?

You say tomato, I say...shut the hell up about tomatoes, already.

I was considering offering some definitions, to possibly explore the distinctions early on in this book between erotica and porn. But in all honesty, when it comes down to the oft-asked question of which is which, I have no idea what the difference is between erotica and porn, and what's more, I'm not even sure there *is* a difference.

Furthermore, if there is one, I'm not sure I give a rat's dingus.

If called on the carpet for a definition, I guess I might offer that, to me, porn feels like more slot-A-into-slot-B kind of stuff, where erotica fills in the gaps between those slots. Still, I really feel this is a subjective eye-of-the-beholder thing, and as Woody Allen said, "If the beholder is blind, just ask the guy next to you."

And again, in the end, I don't think it matters all that much.

Unless a publication you are trying to sell a story to sets a hard and fast distinction with their guidelines, or you know from some past reading of their stuff how intense/detailed and downright dirty your story should or shouldn't be to be published by this press, I wouldn't be too worried about what it is you are scribbling. I have found some publishers or zines that assign a color hierarchy to the erotica they are looking for, as in labeling stories yellow for those that include only 30% naughty sexual action and red for those with kinky stuff amping things up to like 80%. But if you don't find these specifics, don't worry so much about what's coming out of you, whether it be porn, erotica, or something else entirely.

As I advised in the first chapter and will throughout this book, write it, then worry about what it is later.

All too often, I see writers trying to fit their latest opus into a specific category, metaphorically battering the round pegs of what they are writing into the square holes of commercial considerations. Worrying over labeling, thoughts of 'So, what the hell is this, then?' puts unnecessary and all-too-early restrictions on what's supposed to just come pouring out of you. I'm not saying that you shouldn't consider the how/when/where to sell aspects of the game. I'm just advising that you should not worry about what your words might/could/want to be, or stop them if suddenly you find yourself writing what you think is porn when you never thought of writing porn, can't see yourself writing porn, do not WANT TO BE writing porn, on a train, in the rain or in a house with a mouse.

Definitions, labels, and looking for a market for your stuff comes later. You need to have some stuff first.

Let me tell you a little story. I warn you; this is just the first of many, as I will be telling you lots of stories along the way…

E.L. James, the writer of the mega-popular *Fifty Shades of Grey* trilogy, began that saga as fan fiction. She simply let fly her fevered imaginings across an online *Twilight* series fan fiction page. But she learned right quickly though that she couldn't be appropriating the characters from that popular vampire/werewolf series in the way she was if she ever hoped to do more with her scribbling in a professional manner.

Now, I'm not saying there is anything wrong with copying someone's writing style or using settings and characters from your favorite writers to build writing muscle. Have fun, challenge your brain, see what you can come up with, find what works and doesn't work for you. Just don't try and pass these efforts off as original.

Working to excise the *Twilight* peeps and tropes, E.L. recreated her writing as an original tale, and soon…well, the rest is history. The point here is that, although E.L. was metaphorically spanked for what she wrote (and given what she writes about, one could assume the lady might like a good spanking, real or otherwise), James tweaked her first foray into an unimagined success. Now, whether you'd categorize James' super popular, some-would-say-kinky trilogy, erotica, or porn, who cares? What it certainly was, and nobody can debate this, was damn popular and it only ever gained that popularity because the lady took to writing something, be it porn or erotica and wasn't deterred from her first attempts or gave a whit for what it might have been, to have stopped her from writing.

As far as I have been able to tell, we all approach the world and the words we use to describe it through the prisms of our experiences, backgrounds, hopes, dreams, and failures. I couldn't tell you something was pornographic any more that I could decide for you if a hot sauce is too hot for your tastes, and surely, I have read some porn where people use hot sauce in quite interesting ways. The old U.S. Supreme Court has been wrestling with the definition of what porn is for decades, and it seems to me the goalposts move all the time to what one person thinks is objectively filthy as opposed to what another might think merely R-rated.

So, what is erotica, and what is porn? Do you write/read one over the other or both? Who knows? Who cares? Will you write a bunch of one kind of writing and suddenly stop, never to write it again, and go on to something else? Might you balance your output between two or more genres your whole life, or mix and match them consistently? Might you even traipse across both porn and erotica in just one story, something I surely manage to do all the time.

Who cares…just keep writing!

3.

Where Do Ideas Come From?

One of the questions I am asked most frequently, slightly down the list from "So, how does one become a writer?" or "Can you really make a living writing smut?" is "Where do your ideas come from?" The great writer Harlan Ellison used to say that there was a store down on such-a-such street where he used to go and buy his ideas. Oh, dear sweet acerbic Mr. E. I can tell you that be they the stuff of your sexual fantasies, something you have experienced (oh, you lucky bugger, you) or something you might have heard in passing, when you are open to receiving them, little mind noodles of ideas come at you all the time.

Don't follow Ellison's advice and go looking for the idea store. A writer's job is to digest the stuff that comes in, all the time, by any means possible, and spin it to gold.

When my nephew was a little guy, I thought I heard him say "pizza-slipper," which, of course, I stored away for future use. 'Mmm, pizza-slippers,' I thought. He also uttered one of the best quotes I ever heard about my favorite holiday, "Why can't Halloween be every day?" Another idea I stored away.

Sorry, I have copyrights on these. Get your own ideas, you moocher.

As a writer of smut — a writer of anything — really, you are an interloper, audio voyeur, a sneak, a maker-upper of stuff from what you smell, hear, taste, see and feel. Unconsciously, writers fine-tune their five senses so as they walk through the day, they can take stuff in, submerge it into their mind's stew pot, get it to simmer, boil and blanch, even while working at other tasks like driving the kids to a soccer game or giving or taking the high hard one from one's lover. Then some time, whether it be the very next day or a couple of months later, even years from when we first heard that tickle of an idea or enjoyed an experience, our seasoned thoughts are ready to birth something forth to be written.

As you read in my first chapter, my number one advice to would-be writers when they ask me how to start writing is to write. My second piece of advice? Read. Every writer I've ever enjoyed reading was/is a voracious reader. In fact, if you gave me a choice, I'd rather be reading than writing. And while reading is a singular pleasure I have never seen bested, I'd also say that as far as idea gathering goes, reading fills you up just like, and even sometimes more so, than experience.

Again, you are taking in, digesting, and bleeding out the nutrients you need, then coming to use this stuff as the brew you take your writing from.

The thing that's unique to erotica idea gathering is that when you finally get around to writing what you've seasoned in the back alleys of your mind (I was going to say windmills of your mind, but I sold all my windmills years ago for coal burning ovens, which I just wrote here to piss off any conservationists reading me), you reveal yourself in ways other writers do not. When you write about piloting a steaming locomotive being chased by Pony Express robbers, readers immediately take this for the historic-based fantasy it has to be. But have one of those robbers a busty dominatrix? Well, this idea obviously speaks to your more personal prurient interests, you perv!

The revelation of ideas, the meat-and-taters stuff so important to this writing thing we do, brings the naughty writer a bit more scrutiny, as much for the ideas themselves and how well they are executed as the fact that seemingly innocent little you came up with something so nasty.

Lastly, there will come those times that, through writing, you birth wholly new kinks to your experience, fantasy bon mots born right from your head you never thought about or experienced until the moment they bukakke across your page. A scene, setting, or character might be an amalgamation, a mash-up of two or more ideas or people you've met, maybe, something you have done or have yet to try, or people you've imagined in your bed for a very long time. Wherever it all comes from and whatever it turns out to be, as I have always said and will go to my grave shouting: write it, puke it forth, don't worry where your dirty words will leave you (with pants down around your ankles?) or even what they might turn out to be. If you do indeed want those ideas to come, you as much have to be ready and open to take them in as let them out and step out of the way.

Of course, if you don't want to go through any of this, just get in your car and go down to such-and-such street to that store...

4.

Run Silent, Run Niche

I think the farther a writer travels, whether they tickle forth scenes of noir westerns, try their facility at parody romance, or step the way many an erotic writer like me does, fine-tuning BDSM short fiction, they could as much find a rabid audience who will gobble up their specific scribblings, as a broad population who won't give a monkey's banana-stinking fingernail to follow where it is that scribe might be going.

Mixing genres as I often do — marrying smut with satire, science-fiction with kink — has brought me as much forward momentum as it has rejection. Still, I see many a publisher and reader thoroughly enjoying niche material. Later in this book, I interview a writer making a very good living, self-publishing his books, in fact, writing very niche stuff indeed. His is a truly uplifting tale. But I do ask myself time and again, why do we naughty writers seem so often to get all niche-y with it?

Niche, defined as a NOUN, is: "a specialized segment of the market for a particular kind of product or service, as an ADJECTIVE: "denoting or relating to products, services, or **interests** (my bolding) that appeal to a small, specialized section of the population." And maybe, because we naked apes can think up a veritable plethora of stuff (and really, have you ever experienced a plethora that wasn't veritable?) to satisfy our lusts, erotica, the artistic expression of those lusts, is ripe for niche exploration.

As we are all well aware, there's quite a bottomless well to our naughty thoughts, a myriad of specific scenarios we could come to light our thoughts across, more considerations than are in 'heaven and earth' and all that. It stands to reason then that we'd find our way into the wild and weird, the niche in fact, when it comes to the stuff we fantasize over and masturbate to.

And even if it is very specific sexual stuff that you write, there probably is a readership that is into it, too, no matter how niche that itch is that you scratch.

As of this writing, I just placed a story at a male chastity device retailer and am working on more for them. Chastity is undoubtedly a niche kink, but I placed a story at this site, a site with a healthy readership. I was prompted to write this niche story following some instinct to delve a little deeper into what became, in my story, a teasing/fem dom/power-play dynamic. And yet again I found that there are others who think about, and enjoy stories that engage, this niche-y noodle of an idea.

I know how it is, believe me. You sit in your home-based writer's garret, hunkered over your keyboard, trying to work out exactly how to get what's in your head out of your fingers, so it makes some sense when it's read. And in the mental wrestling over plots, places, and the people of your making, all pretty much born whole cloth from your imaginings, you toil, edit, and maybe even search for markets for your work.

But you come to doubt yourself, as all writers do, ruminating over the worry of who will really will ever want to read your scribbling. You think you should chuck it all to try your hand at more lucrative types of writing (and hey, when you find these more lucrative types, let me know about them, okay?) or you start down that windy road of amortizing the time you spent writing against the monetary return for your endeavors and grow so disgusted with what you did not make, yet again, and how you have twisted yourself in knots just to get the next sentence right, that you give up writing entirely.

As my friend Tom (whom you will meet later) and I discuss all the time, as he toils to write comedy routines and jokes, and me whatever it is that I have come up against presently that is driving me crazy: it is less the doing of the thing that is frustrating as it is always more the doubt that comes rushing over you almost all of the time that, in the end, no one is going to care anyway that you did the thing.

Add into all this that you find yourself writing the oddest, most specific kind of drivel, niche stuff to the tenth power; believe me, I can see why you might have a moment of passing hopelessness! But don't give up. I am constantly amazed at the niche stuff that sells, across erotica, sci-fi, and so much genre writing.

To paraphrase a *Field Of Dreams*-ism, "If you write it, they might indeed cum." And in the case of the naughty niche writer, I might just mean this, literally.

If it be niche, then let there be niche, my brothers and sisters.

5.

Shooting Up The Old Mental Enema
To Relieve Your Writer's Block

This is one of the areas of writing (and there are many, believe me) where I am not very learned. I just never suffer from the all-too-common, wheels-spinning-in-the-mud mind-lockdown of writer's block. Sure, I suffer from the lazies. I'll do all I can to avoid sitting down to write, put off a project even if it has a deadline, find anything else to do but start working. But, for the most part, I have so many projects needing completion — and it's less work for employers than it is my own stuff — that flittering from one page to a wholly different one keeps my mental muscles in such snapping shape so I don't get stuck or blocked.

Of course, I'm not saying I get much done this way. In fact, I probably get less work done on one specific thing than if I were to concentrate on one piece of writing and didn't start another until I finished the first. But I get bored quickly, especially in my work, and writing this way is the way I have always done it, lighting across a whole bunch of stuff at the same time.

But even though I do not suffer from writer's block, I know it exists. Plenty of writers do suffer it from time to time, some lots more than others. So, I offer the following five prompts to maybe get you a' flowing?

Number one: Push yourself back from your desk, get away from what you are trying to slog through, and take a break from writing. Getting your mind off the work and your ass out of your chair is the first and best solution. No matter how much desire for writing you have, how it might be your bread and butter, you need a break, as does anyone else doing any other job.

Isaac Asimov was famous for declaring that writing gave him the best vacation. The far-off worlds he conjured and the characters he created took him lightyears away from his worries and life. Still, all Asimovian considerations aside (and really, there was only ever one Isaac Asimov), I feel the first real way to break through your block is to break away from writing.

Two: You could try to plow through by assigning yourself writing of a wholly different nature than what you are presently stuck on. Mired deep in trying to write your latest bodice-ripper? Open up a new document and try to pen an article on fly fishing. All but exhausted re-reading the same second-act of your three-act opus? Start a blog. What often gets us hitting the wall, beyond burn-out, is that we have been attempting to do the same kind of writing for too long. Sure, starting some other writing might be damn hard when you might not be writing at all, even counterproductive when you should be working to meet a deadline. But, if you can't or do not want to step away from the laptop or desk, ok, then keep writing. But try writing something different, or even opposite to what's got you stuck.

Three: For this one, you are going to have to truly take a break: go and read. As I have mentioned before, reading is one of my favorite pursuits, the best vacation, as powerful and vital to me as any actual trip I have ever taken. It cleans out my cobwebs, sets me traveling, and feeds me the words and techniques of other scribes. Besides writing, I find reading is the best activity to get me writing anew.

Four: Find a writer's support group, conference, hang, or class. You won't get far from the idea/talk/the very smell of writing, but sometimes just being around others suffering through similar daily conundrums — and God knows writer's block isn't the only worry a writer can have — might help.

As I wrote before, my good buddy, podcast co-host, co-teacher of my classes and fantastic writer M. Christian knows me in a specific way like nobody else, as much because we are such good friends as that he is an erotica writer just like me and fully understands my daily trials and tribulations. When I speak to Chris, I can unburden, as much as he can and does with me, the writing worries we have, so often similar, in a 'misery loves company' cleansing. Being with other writers you can unload with a group of like-minded folks who understand and can support your particular woes as you do theirs.

Five: Imbibe. Start pounding the drink. Take up the sauce like Dylan Thomas, the opium, like Edgar Allen Poe the...I'm joking. I don't recommend or ingest any stimulant or hallucinogen to loosen writer's block. Although, if *Funny Bones* or *Yodels* count, then maybe I have a problem with imbibing my own particular poisons.

Don't blot out your brain with substances; it's not going to end well. And post 30, being out of it is really not a good look.

Try everything above, save the last. One, two, or maybe all four will get you through the log jam. I hope something does. I have heard that writer Aaron Sorkin takes multiple showers during the day; somehow, warming his body warms his talent to keep flowing. I am sure you have heard about plenty of writers who go for the old walk around the block or those that take in a round of handball with a bud. I don't know what will work for you, but four of the above are worth trying.

I just hope whatever mental enema you choose, it keeps you unblocked for a long time.

Don't Burn That Confounded Bridge

Here is the first of a few chapters in this book that doesn't precisely deal with writing but is more about one's behavior while working at or selling writing. But what I explore here is an important point and one that you'll see me come back to time and again, and as such, I think it deserves its own chapter. I will give you a ton of examples below and all through these pages about how you should *never burn a bridge*.

As we are all aware, it is so very easy these days to register a complaint. All you have to do is tweet, spit out an email, or get up on TikTok about some slight you've felt or injustice you think has slip-slid your way. But just because we can do something, and might even feel justified in doing it, doesn't mean we should. This is especially true when slogging off some employer, giving a co-worker a piece of your mind, or letting a publisher or editor know of your displeasure. I advise, almost at every turn, quietly suffering the slings and arrows coming your way and keeping quiet.

If you absolutely feel compelled to address the person you feel wronged you, take a breath before you do, even write out your email or tweet, but ***do not send it***. Let it lie; come back to it later. Often our anger subsides over time for a more reasoned read of the problem, and we come to regret sending something we dashed off in the first blush of anger. If after sufficient and sure consideration you still want to let your missive fly, well, at least, you can always satisfy yourself that you were mature enough not to go off half-cocked.

Generally speaking, I don't think it's ever a good idea to "put your shit out there," cocked or not. It's just not mature to whine, which is really what sending emails, posting, tweeting over this kind of thing is. And I can assure you, mostly these days, the person who hurt your feelings or you feel disrespected by will barely, if at all, care about what you have to say. Don't be offended by this, it's just that most folks are just so concerned with their little microcosmic view of existence through their cell phones, that they barely register anyone else's existence anyway. Really. Haven't you noticed? Maybe you are locked nose-deep into your own cell phone too often to have noticed.

And hell, even if your complaint registers really the most your comeback will engender is more vitriol and an excuse for the person you complained to, to tweet, vlog, Tikity-Tokity or share your displeasure with their friends.

And we all know, once we put something up on the web, it stays forever.

And lastly, your crying, certainly contradicts my suggestion of not burning a bridge.

Let's face it, you simply do not know when your current status with someone, good or bad, could change in a way that might line your pockets…even fill your bed. Keeping on good terms with everybody, best that you can, you might find a friend where you once thought you only would ever have an enemy. Or, at the very least, someone who might be able to give you something you want or need. Sure, people who need people "are the luckiest people," and all that, but there often are completely selfish reasons for maintaining good relationships.

Here's a very real example of this that, as of this writing, just happened to me.

I was writing for a magazine that did not pay me (in the next chapter, I address the many reasons why even a professional might take a job that doesn't pay). But there came a moment between the CEO/editor of this magazine and me when I felt that I was at least owed something very basic because a.) at the very least, I thought I'd see this one morsel come my way because I was *not* getting paid and b.) what I was asking for he had already provided in the previous instances of the magazine's publication, and c.) providing me with this would have been the decent thing to do. I made my point, and only to the person I should have made my point to, and politely I might add, and…we moved on. Fast forward a few months, and the editor/CEO of this magazine just let me know that he now has the resources to pay his writers. So, in keeping my cool, not burning this particular bridge, when I rightly felt I was nearly justified to, I now have a paying gig.

I could pepper this chapter with even more examples, like when someone suddenly came to me, years from the last time we spoke, with a new work opportunity. I had not been in touch with this person for a while, but because we were always cordial, and I did an excellent job for him way back, he came to find me and offered me a new job. In my life, these instances happen so often that I'd calculate referrals count for about 60% of the jobs I get. Or how about the times one employer has recommended me to another because that first employer not only liked my work but felt I was a decent enough fellow and was always nice to them (see Patrick Swayze later on in this book). Or, the case of me suffering a slew of rejections from none other than M. Christian, that led to us becoming fast friends and co-workers.

Actually, how Chris and I grew to be besties is a fun story, and surely illustrates the don't burn a bridge axiom. Allow me to digress...

Way before meeting him, Chris edited and owned a blog called "Frequently Felt." It was a daily online depository of naughty ideas, essays, poetry, what have you that lots of people took to and writers like me submitted to regularly. But at first, for a good half-a-year, Chris rejected pretty much everything I sent him. He was always kind enough to shoot off a quick email of how the most recent piece I had sent in just didn't hit the mark with what he was looking for, but to keep trying.

I finally broke through, getting up to speed with the style of writing Chris was after (or he just finally came to his senses) and he came to take plenty of my future essays, poems and little missives. If I had stopped sending my pieces to Chris, simply said, "Forget him; he obviously has his taste up his arse," even railed back and burned a bridge with the guy, we would never have grown to be the good friends and co-workers we are today.

Actually, in Chris's defense, I'm sure even if I had slogged him off, he wouldn't have dismissed me out of hand; he's just not that kind of a guy. Frankly, neither am I. But the point is, if I had lit the kindling under the expanse here, let the rickety bridge I was trying to build go up in flames, I might have never experienced one of the true great friendships I have cultivated in my later years.

I'll give you more examples.

There are some writers that I don't particularly like. It's not a question of our styles not meshing; there are just some people who I do not get along with, hard as I try. And, there are plenty of people who don't get along with me. I know, I know, this is hard to believe, who wouldn't get along with little old peaches-and-cream, me? But on more than one occasion, I've recommended one or two of these writers I do not like for a job I was offered but knew I couldn't do. To my way of thinking, it's stupid to let my feelings get in the way of business, especially when there's no business for me to be had. To quote *The Godfather*, "It's not personal; it's only business." And if you want to attribute a little nefarious underpinning to my recommendations, there have been those occasions where I recommended a writer to an employer, when both that writer and/or the employer have come back to recommend me for a job or hired me.

How 'bout more one example?

Like with all my writing, I send the various children' books my buddy/ illustrator and I have created far and wide. I might read about a small press suddenly open to submissions or find an agent I can try and tickle with one of our silly books. About a half a year ago from this writing I found and reached out to a UK publisher of kids' books.

To my amazement, the main guy at the company took to our titles, to one specifically, and it seemed we were on our way. But within a few weeks this guy emailed me some terrible news about his personal life which impinged on the financing he was counting on to keep the press going. I thanked the man for his time and agreed that I would indeed try him in the New Year as he wanted, but having been on this kind of precipice many times, I didn't hold too much hope for any true purchase for further climbing. But I never thought, even for a blip of a second, to burn this bridge, tell the guy to go scratch, etc.

Guess who just got in touch with me, coffers full again, looking to revitalize his imprints and wants to talk about the book we left on the table?

I can go on and on about this point. It is essential in developing, maintaining, and building your reputation and in overall better networking. So, please, even if you feel an aching desire to, are assured that you are justified, want to enact some revenge on somebody you just know has obviously wronged you or simply would rather just "ghost" someone: don't burn any confounded bridges you happen to make.

7.

Did You Get Paid? How Much Did You Get Paid? Why Didn't You Get Paid?

Having mentioned him once already, you should realize I am a big fan of Harlan Ellison. Running through Amazon Prime just recently, I caught a documentary on the great man called "Dreams with Sharp Teeth." It's an in-depth look at this amazing writer's career, with some great interviews with him, Neil Gaiman, and other writers, plus some hilarious interplay between Ellison and Robin Williams. There is no way you can watch this film and not realize how important Ellison thinks the written word is and how strongly he feels writers should value (and get paid for) what they do.

This fantastic fantasist, writer for "Star Trek," "The Outer Limits," and scores of short stories, essays, criticism, screenplays, etc., offers a strong argument about how writers who work for free devalue the art/work of writing. On the surface, Ellison is correct. But there is something to be considered here that I feel Mr. E. missed in his ranting. Coming from the high-end of the scale where he was and having enjoyed his beginnings as a short story writer when short story writers could indeed make enough to live on, Ellison is not taking into account the times we live in (the documentary was made in 2008) nor the fact that, in some cases, a writer might still want to write for someone even knowing that they will not get paid in the current coin of the realm.

If I received a payment for the number of times somebody has asked me, "So, what did they pay you for this?" or "How much did you make off this book?" and "You didn't get paid? Why the hell did you do the job then?" I'd be a very rich man indeed. But the simple fact is, even as the professional that I am, I sometimes get paid my asking price, I sometimes get paid not what I would have liked, and plenty of times, I don't get paid at all…at least not monetarily.

Let's take these three points one by one and I'll explain why sometimes I agree with each.

When I get paid: Yippee, see Ralph make money! See Ralph buy shit he doesn't need (beyond food, shelter, etc.). See Ralph feel validated by an employer who thinks his talent and time are worth something. See a happy Ralph.

Getting paid what you're worth or what you've asked? Yes, it's great and in a perfect world, this should be how it always is. But you can't count on this always happening when you work as a freelance writer. Woefully unfair? Devaluing the profession? Sure. But I can assure you, no matter what level of writer you are, sometimes there just isn't money to pay you for your work, or a lot less than your usual asking price. So, then, why take the work?

Read on…

When I get paid less than I have liked/wanted/asked: See, Ralph happy to have still made a buck. See, Ralph maybe working at a lesser amount than he usually would have gotten for many reasons — infiltrating a company heretofore closed to me, but slipping in because I priced myself so cheap (at first), or the work is so much fun I don't mind making a little less, or working for a buddy — and see Ralph fully aware of what he signed up for. And if the lesser pay bugs Ralph too much after a while (or the other rewards are not forthcoming as Ralph had been promised), see Ralph quit this job.

When I don't get paid…money: See Ralph working for a whole host of other reasons.

I might acquire product. I might be looking to build my reputation or some credits with a particular type of writing I haven't done before. Again, I might be working for a bud or, this might be an opportunity to set up a recurring column/blog/interview platform all on my own, which has happened to me on many occasions and led to contacts and even more work. Non-paying work has even led to me creating this book, as I mentioned when I told you about my sexpert.com column, a column I wrote for free.

Now, as much as I won't immediately turn down a gig that does not pay in money or pays less than I usually get, I also won't immediately take a job that pays more than I typically see. "What?! Ralph, are you crazy!" I hear you say.

Sure, I can be bought as much as anybody. I am easily waylaid by a shiny object or somebody tickling my vanity, and by 'vanity' I mean…

What I am trying to hammer home to you here is that you need to weigh every instance on its own merit, have it one. I have been on the receiving end of what seemed like an excellent salary but came to detest the work, or the employer became too difficult over time that I had to quit the job. Yes, it struck me deep in my bottom line to walk away in these lucrative instances. The money was great. The place I was writing for was well known. I would have bolstered my resume. But the problems with each employer caused me so much aggravation that no amount I was being paid would make up for the agita.

Of course, none of this answers the other big questions that surface when money is involved; how much should you charge if a budget is not set, or if the possible client puts the onus on you to give them a figure of how much you will charge? And what recourse do you have if you don't get paid what you were promised or don't get paid at all?

Let me take this last point first: you didn't get paid.

Well, you're kinda SOL, Ranger Rick.

Sure, you can start a schmear campaign online, let your fellow writers know about your experiences, yawp your troubles across the https:// writersweekly.com/ email newsletter. If the writing job is one you went to an actual office for, sure, you can confront somebody there, but as most of what I do is remote (and I am sure it is for you too), other than incendiary emails, texts, and tweets, which can all too easily be turned around and considered harassment, how do you shake your money loose?

Before I did this writing thing full time, I worked for my father in his commercial collection agency. We'd hear all the time from clients, "Well, if they won't pay us, I'll just sue!" We'd have to advise clients constantly that suing somebody for a measly $300.00 would cost time and money. Even if you were to enter a civil lawsuit, even sans lawyer, you have to pay court costs and filing fees; these add up, not to mention the time away from work you have to spend attending court in whatever county the debtor resides in.

It just wasn't worth it.

The same rule or expenditure of time and money applies to us lowly scribes. Unless you have an iron-clad contract with an employer and the amount they owe you is considerable, paying a lawyer to enforce your contract, prove you did the work that you say you did, then actually get your money might not be worth your time and money.

To the other points about payment: As with most everything else these days, you can find plenty of formulas for calculating your payment-to-word-count ratio or what a writer of your experience can expect to make given the current marketplace. You can also manage a sufficient search across the net about a potential new employer to try and determine how deep their pockets might be. But in the end, just because you can determine your hourly rate via some online calculation or even by talking to a colleague, it doesn't mean you still shouldn't determine the amount you want on a case-by-case basis or be so set on a number you beg off a good job.

Let me give you two recent examples from my life on how the above point works from each side of the what-I-should-be-getting/what-I-want-to-get coin (haha, I wrote the word 'coin' when we are talking about money here, did you catch how clever I am?)

An agent I had worked with a while ago, somebody who hits me up across Skype every so often, or I'll send a *Hey, how you doin'?* to every couple of months, left me a message that he had a new job for which he thought I might be suitable. I had worked about a year-and-a-half on a project for this guy where I had to employ six other writers to handle a massive workload. I made some money, got to spread a little cash around to some freelancers I knew who could use it and had some fun traveling a bit for the job.

It also made me crazy because I was locked at the computer all the time and, quite frankly, was scrambling to produce more content than was probably healthy for me, all because I was being paid so little I had to make it up in volume. But, hey, I signed up for it. I knew what I was getting myself into, and at the time, I needed the dough badly.

The new job the guy presented? Well, the price for the work was, again, way too low. But these days, ten years on from the last job I did for him, my circumstances are a bit better (or maybe I give less of a shit), and I can choose to be slightly pickier with whatever work comes in (slightly). I countered with what I felt was a very reasonable "family rate," but he couldn't budge from the pittance he was offering. So, I declined.

Ok, nobody got hurt, and the agent and I remain friends. Actually, he made it easier for me because I know the bare minimum I have to make, seeing as there wouldn't be any other kind of compensation, and he couldn't get himself up even to this amount. There was no question in my mind; I simply couldn't do the work. And even though I genuinely don't/didn't/won't, ever have a set price to keep me from work, I still knew enough that I couldn't work for what he was offering.

Conversely, a good buddy of mine put feelers out to gather together some writers for a new project she was helming. Not to toot my own ram's too loudly, but the work fell well within my wheelhouse. There was the added bonus that my friend and I get along great, and there was no worry about getting paid here. The pay, though, wasn't great, well below what I'd generally ask, not as bad as the example above, but still very low.

But I took the job. Why? Because of the many positive factors in the sentences above; I could do the work with my eyes closed (though I don't recommend writing with your eyes closed), the person employing me was a good friend, and I knew there would never be a question about getting paid. But if I were one of those writers who have a firm, non-negotiable rate, I would never have taken this job.

I can't weigh the factors, salary, whatever else you consider when taking this or that job. I can't advise you on what price you should set for your services. And I certainly can't determine what type of non-monetary compensation might hold worthwhile value to you. All I can say is, weigh every job and know that your compensation might not just be about money in every instance, as much as, sometimes, money is all you should be considering. And sorry, Harlan, but I don't think a writer devalues writing by charging whatever they charge, in any way they charge it, and even when they do not get paid for work they do.

8.
Spread 'Em

I went to see Kurt Vonnegut lecture in the mid-'80s. Being one of my all-time most favorite authors, you can bet I was thrilled to be among the sold-out crowd in that college auditorium that weekday night back in the days of my mid-twenties when I was fancy foot and so free. All of us digesting every word the master said, I clearly remember one of the points the urbane Mr. V. was adamant about. He regaled us all that when he was first starting to write and publish, a fledgling author could find a whole host of places to send stories, essays, and poetry. These places would pay to place all kinds of genre fiction into the pages of what were almost always professional magazines well respected in their fields. Some were indeed fiction mags, while others would run one or two stories in an issue alongside the rest of their usual non-fiction fare. What dearly departed Mr. Vonnegut didn't have to tell us that night, although he did, was that these free range-like publication opportunities did not so much exist anymore.

These many years on, surely, it could be argued that with the advent of the internet, there are more places than ever before to get your stuff out to. But the possibility these days of placing a story in a pro magazine or print quarterly journal, or even on that same publication's online portal, takes a sure amount of searching. And go ahead, show me a quarterly print journal like *The Paris Review* or a mainstream mag like *The New Yorker*, publishing genre fiction. And erotica? Come on Scooby Doo, there's no mystery to how few naughty stories these places publish.

An erotica writer who wants to be published these days needs to familiarize him or herself with the fine art of 'spreading.'

Yes, in writing dirty stuff, we know all about spreading; legs, libido, desires, and the spray of leather tethers across the wet, waiting, and warm body spots of various partners. But for the point I am making here, I suggest spreading your scribbling as far and wide as possible.

Writing market sites like Duotrope.com will lead you to publication site guidelines and the wonderful array of anthologies currently looking; they also showcase agents and defunct publications.

Signing up for a daily round-up of places looking for writing on a specific Patreon page is also a good idea (I have scored lots of jobs this way). You can also check out https://writersweekly.com/; as previously mentioned. I also find https://www.erotica-readers.com/ a spectacular resource.

It also helps to spread your output around to different publishers other than the ones you usually publish with. Sure, the prevailing wisdom is to build a relationship with one publisher by growing a healthy listing of books with them, so they start to consider you a worthwhile commodity, a part of the family. But there is also something to be said for placing a bunch of titles with a bunch of different publishers.

Admittedly, this isn't so easy to do with a niche like erotica, where the pickings of potential publishers are few, but a long time ago, the wonderful and wise Jean Marie Stine of Renaissance ebooks, the first house to publish my erotica in complete book form, and the place I go back to time and again, told me that it was a good idea to have a bunch of books published by a bunch of different houses. In her wise and caring view, J.M. didn't see this as competition as much as free advertising, in that if someone found and enjoyed a book of mine published by one house, they might go looking for more titles by me, and that search might very well bring them to my books published by Jean Marie.

Makes sense, right?

If you are a short fiction writer, you might also consider the idea of 'spreading' a bunch of stories into one themed collection to fill an entire book, which is what I did in my first initial offerings with Jean Marie. If you are of a mind, and it seems your words can take the slicing and dicing, you can also take whole chapters of a longer novel, revise them a bit and maybe have this edit published as a shorter piece on a webzine or in an antho. As I've told you before, don't be so stuck on what you think the thing before you *has to* be. You might be able to reimagine, shorten or add to it, so it becomes altogether something else, or in the end, you might get two things out of one just by your editing.

Then there are the many audio book publishers out there looking for either full novels, or short story collections, and there are podcasts also looking to read fiction on air. So, search for these opportunities as well.

Also, there is Amazon. I'll get into the good and bad of self-publishing in a later chapter, specifically on Jeff Bezos' massive, all-encompassing portal. But suffice it to say, you can pretty much put up anything on Amazon, although with erotica, I can't promise you it will stay put up (again, more on this later).

The first and best advocate for your scribbling is always going to be you, despite what an agent might say or a publisher might promise. And these days there seems to be so much out there for the taking, and I certainly emphasize the 'seems to be' part of this sentence. As we know, things are not always what they truly are out there on that wacky Interweb thingie, as much as there are a great many publishing houses being held together by smoke and mirror, only ever self-publishing one book by the sole owner/author of that press.

Get up on all fours, metaphorically speaking, thrust your fanny in the air and spread 'em, but do some good research.

9.

The Conundrum Over Rewriting or 'Know When To Hold'em,' Know When To Fold'em'

Here are two quotes, one an oldie-but-goodie and one I just found; both have been rattling 'round my brain lately.

Ernest Hemingway's "The only kind of writing is rewriting," from *A Moveable Feast* and "Write for yourself, edit for your audience," from…I don't know where.

Both, I dare say, make lots of sense. But both are infinitely dangerous and could lead many a well-reasoned or even long-seasoned writer down a rabbit hole from which they might never crawl back.

Let's take on Papa H. first.

When not chasing bulls or looking for fights, Hemingway was undoubtedly (or arguably, take your pick) writing and rewriting some of the most powerful fiction ever produced. But I disagree with his quip here and would have arm-wrestled the bearded scribe about it had we met.

Yes, rewriting is essential to writing. Unless one happens to be Isaac Asimov, the granddaddy of modern science fiction, who did not rewrite, his amazing stuff flowing perfectly as he typed it; rare case that he was. But I have always thought writing is the act of puking forth *without* revising. It happens best when one doesn't think and just lets things flow without regard for form, editing, or audience, as I have written here plenty already. So, no, Ernie H., I'd have to revise your quote to, "Writing is writing."

This is no small point. I am not just playing with semantics. If a writer takes the tack that the only kind of writing *is* rewriting, they will be forever looking ahead, ignoring what they put down first, and muck up the process of getting it down over what it might be later.

The second quote...

If we are trying to stay true to this art-making-thing-via-writing, then the art that we make, be it writing a poem, sculpting, weeding our garden, or baking a cake, needs to be made for ourselves first and foremost because we have the burning need to make it. The audience for our art can indeed come into the equation, we might even want to consider them, but here again, I say step with caution.

Surely, you've heard the stories of contradictory Hollywood movie previews. An out-of-town showing of a yet-to-be-released film summons forth a post-show review card barrage of terrible criticism, leaving director, producer, writer, and even actors devastated. But then the same movie plays the following week in another town, and it's a rave.

The creator of a thing can't trust the hive mind of an audience to influence decisions on what they give that audience. As much as one should step very gingerly indeed when starting to slice and dice their prose/play/poem for an audience they have in mind or for a trend they are currently trying to ride.

For example, I have sat at multiple showings of one of my one-acts, to find an audience roaring with laughter at one line of dialogue one night, and the next night, that same line, delivered in the same way by the same actor, only elicits a low chuckle from one person. Yes, I have revised my plays for actors or a director even, especially when I hear lines up and running and realize how clunky they might be, but I don't edit for what I think an audience may or may not take to.

Surely, collaboration, be it with a fellow writer, actors and directors bringing your play to life, or working with an editor, is a whole different animal. If you are working with someone, or, as mentioned before, being paid to write something specific, you need to act according to the parameters you set up for that work. But publishing or presenting your words to a readership or audience needs to be taken on a case-by-case basis, as with all we do in life. Editing for what you *think* an audience might like is pretty much a tail-wagging-the-dog scenario, as much as you can start that dog's tail by setting your mind to rewriting before you even start writing.

Which leads to us considering the "when to hold'em, when to fold'em" in this equation. In other words, *when should we stop rewriting?*

1.) *When you grow bored with what you've written.* Let's assume you have already done some deep-dive rewriting on your piece. You put it aside, come back to it a few days later, and give it repeated floggings... and really, what one of us doesn't like a repeated flogging? But on the fourth, fifth or seventy-eighth time back on it, if you find you are more than bored with the thing, it might be time to say it's finished and send it out or at least let somebody else read it.

 And let me tell you, if you don't grow aroused any longer over a piece of erotica that came sluicing out your head, you are as much done reading it as you are done writing it.

2.) *When, whoever you let read what you wrote, reacts favorably to what you wrote.* This is a sticky wicket, to be sure — "Eww, your wicket is all sticky!"

Like the aforementioned movie studios passing out comment cards at test screenings, each person's opinion is simply, each person's opinion. But if you trust the person you happen to give your piece to, mostly agree with their sensibilities, and they happen to react positively, maybe even have to beg off for a quick one-handed tickle after reading a naughty few pages you wrote, this might be all the proof you need that you've done your job.

3.) *When you need to meet a deadline.* This one lets you off the hook or adds pressure; take your pick. But for those of us writing to a deadline, especially to get paid, we will only ever be granted a finite amount of rewriting.

4.) *When the thing you are writing morphs into something else.* Again, this is a hard one to navigate as sometimes we are as much unaware this is happening as unconsciously resistant. But it's not so bad if your short story starts to unfurl itself into a novelette or that poem prompts you to pluck its wry rhyming meat and starts you scribbling a one-act play from its lines. The fine point here is: A.) if something wants to become something else, let it. B.) if in becoming something else, it might keep you rewriting in some form, that's ok, and C.) you might end up with two (or more things) if the first thing — follow me here, it gets a little bumpy — feels like it might want to be something else and you can keep from not completely trashing that first thing for the new thing it seems to have become.

5.) *When you damn well want to.* No small point, and it does not really have to do with any of the above. Sometimes you just come to a point in the rewriting where you're not bored, you don't have a deadline, you haven't shared the piece with anybody else, and the thing you are writing is just as it has always been and has not flipped into being something else. But, still, you simply want to stop rewriting because you…just…want…to. It's not a case of laziness. It's not you looking to simply get up out of your chair to do something else. It's just that you look at the thing you are writing and think: 'Mmmm, great spinning orb of the galaxy, I just don't wanna do this rewriting thing anymore.' Listen to this voice, sometimes it is best to do its bidding.

Editing, revising, walking away for a while, coming back, reassessing, damning the muse, shooting wide and not hitting a target, working backward and suddenly finding one, this is all part and parcel of writing; yes, what is called rewriting. And I love this part, I really do, and I certainly agree that it is crucial. But as much as anybody else, I can get stuck in revising, the cutting and pasting, and spend whole days agonizing over the use of one word over another. What you are doing here is essential, sure, but don't let it become a Sisyphean task, a Whac-A-Mole scene you can't extricate yourself from (sorry for the two metaphors back to back. Maybe I should have revised better here?)

Remember, rewriting is *not* writing.

10.
Go Out And Get That Job, Bucko!

Years ago, I interviewed the fantastic actor Frankie Faison. A nicer guy you'd never meet. He was promoting a movie at the time, and I was allowed about fifteen minutes with the affable Mr. F. Besides playing "Barney" in the various Hannibal Lecter franchise of movies. Mr. Faison was also in one of my favorite all-time flicks, the Keith Gordon-directed — another talented dude you should go searching for — film version of dearly-departed Kurt Vonnegut's *Mother Night*. In talking with Mr. Faison, he told me that although he was a sought-after character actor with a good amount of work to his credit and more coming, he was always looking for more work.

Let that be a lesson to you and me.

Shifting slightly forward from my 'Spread 'em' chapter, I can advise that it's probably a good idea to keep a fire slightly kindling under your butt, have you the need to make a living from this writing thing. I don't rightly know why or even when a sudden burst of motivation will take me, although I wish it took me more often. But I know I put myself out there more and more these days. Just recently, I landed a client in Russia, far from my wild N.J, suburban environs, by cold calling (cold emailing, actually), something I don't so readily do, but desperate times and all that. Although, as a freelancer, all times are desperate.

In this case, I reached out because I happened to receive a weekly newsletter emailer from this adult toy company and figured, how could it hurt just to say hello and introduce myself, see if, indeed, they might be looking for copywriters. It took months for me to score an interview/consideration/manage a Skype call with the woman I began emailing back and forth and then the CEO of the company.

Since I had inserted myself unsolicited into their world, and there had been a slow courtship of "Do we need this guy?" "Maybe we do indeed need this guy?""How do we facilitate even considering this guy?" I waited patiently over the two months it took to manage that Skype contact. Sure, I checked in via email and readied further links and my resume until they called, but it came down to the proverbial "Don't call us; we'll call you."

The lessons I learned?

Reach out, even if there is no actual job posting. You might just hit someone at the very moment they are looking for what you do, without maybe even realizing that they need someone to do what you do. Also, stay persistent, but do not cross over into annoying. Surely, this is not always a balance you can easily manage or even can determine the parameters of. But these days with email, Skype, digital carrier pigeon, Zoom-Zoom-Zoomity, you can maintain a respectful 'just-checking-in-to-see-if-you-have-anything-for-me' distance. This also works for those jobs you already have or those people you only occasionally work for; keep on them, but softly, Ms. Flack.

There's also lots to be learned and sometimes even gained, taking a meeting or managing a few back-and-forth emails for a job that might not exactly be in your wheelhouse or that you find, initially, might not exactly pay what you are looking for. Here's yet another example from my recent work searching and something that makes the point on this point:

I found a call for writers on a sex job board, called Sexyjobs.com (clever right?) and sent an email. All too quickly though I learned from contacting the would-be employer, a lovely husband and wife team, that they didn't have the budget to afford my services, reasonable as my prices are, against the rest of what they needed to spend their money on. But I pushed the couple to at least make some time for a phone call with me, secretly hoping that we could come to some middle ground where they could throw me a little work, and they'd still have money left for the rest of what they needed to get done. I was also ready to come in under my usual price, as I usually am, if things felt right. Punting though I was, the couple seemed like honest folk, had a pretty cool service model, and quite frankly, a freelancer can't afford to be so cavalier to let potential work flitter past just because things don't fit perfectly as planned during an initial contact.

What I found talking to the couple was that, indeed, I could do the work needed and, in doing so, eliminate a further piece of the equation they thought they needed, and had budgeted for but, with me onboard, would be encompassed in what I delivered. In other words, they could save the money they were going to spend on another writer and siphon a little of this budget over to me. I am not always the 'fixer' in every situation, but I do have a particular set of skills that can sometimes land me a job and (although my particular set of skills will never get my daughter away from kidnappers, I'd have to rely on good old Liam for that) by saving an employer worry, time, and some bucks.

There's a line from the movie *Glengarry Glen Ross* that I've morphed to fit my philosophy regarding looking for/pursuing work. In that movie, Alec Baldwin's character berates the salesmen he oversees with an "Always be closing" call to action. Freelance writers, I feel, should "Always be looking."

I am also reminded of a story I heard from my dear, old dad, who worked part-time at his uncle's garage when he was in his early 20s. Soaking up mechanical knowledge as much as life wisdom from the older guys who'd come in to have their cars serviced and stick around to have a jaw, Dad told me about a chauffeur who came in occasionally. As it surely was his livelihood, decades before the ubiquitous Uber or Lyft, the guy had to make sure his big Caddy was in top shape, so he was in often.

On one of his regular visits, the chauffeur related to my father how one time he made an airport run to pick up the iconic comedian Henny Youngman, forever known for his classic "Take my wife…please," one-liner (YouTube him if you're unfamiliar). Henny was scheduled for a gig at the famed NYC Waldorf Astoria hotel, but as the driver began to take Henny to The Big Apple, the comedian requested that he be driven to a spot somewhere in northern New Jersey. Henny wanted to run in, and do an hour at some small out-of-the-way local hall in one of our smaller 'burbs. Amiable as Youngman was during the drive, he and the chauffeur got to talking, and the driver asked the great comedian why he was stopping off to do what was obviously, a smaller and a lesser paying gig, before his more significant NYC engagement.

"Why go out of your way?" the driver asked.

"If I can manage it, I never turn down an opportunity to make money," Henny explained.

And, to reiterate a point I made in chapter six, I'm sure Henny Youngman had a price in mind for how little he would take for this gig, but he decided that this NJ stop-off, even though paying less than his usual asking, was worth his time.

Of course, there is a codicil to all this persistent job hunting, job landing, and job working. In your daily courting new clients, jumping into projects even if the pay ain't so great, hunting down a brittle lead through some past networking, sometimes, you could find yourself with too much work. Surely, this doesn't happen all that often, and it's an enviable position to be in. Still, while trying to free your eggs from Pudd'nhead's basket warning (see Mark Twain for that reference) you might just line yourself up for an amount of work you simply can't get to.

Again, this is not a regular occurrence for too many of us, if ever at all. But when it happens that you suddenly have too much work on your plate, and you can't make your deadlines, you'll have to prioritize, assess what jobs you need to put your immediate attention to, figure what of all you do will make you the most…in money, attention, establishing a foothold in a company or courting the boss's daughter or son. During the handful of times I have come up against this conundrum, I made my calculations best I could, working hard not to completely sever the lines of communication with the employer I was turning down so they might remember me fondly at a later date. It was just another example of that golden rule of never burning a bridge.

Remember what the great Lee Strasberg says as Hyman Roth in *The Godfather, Part II* (although he is talking about organized crime and the origins of Las Vegas) "This, *ktch*, is the business we've chosen."

And unless you have an agent who makes their ten to fifteen percent off the jobs they bring you or a ride-'til-they-die editor you know who will throw you work all the time, as a freelancer, you need be out there constantly overturning rocks looking for the jobs that might be hiding underneath.

11.

5 Ideas For The Erotica Writer's Writing Routine

I can't tell you when, where, or how to write any more than you could tell me. As mine do, your writing time, place, and habits have to work for you. Everybody's output is different, as are our styles and routines. But what I impart here are five ideas that I feel might work for all of us, no matter the when/where/how, or what we write, for a better writing routine.

1.) **Find/create a delineated space to write in.** This one is not so easy to come by or create, especially if you are just starting to scribble, are a part-timer, or live in a busy household. It might be tough to squirrel away a specific space all your own, apart from the family or your romantic partner, someplace quiet where you can dream or secluded enough that you can blast the Emerson, Lake and Palmer at all hours for inspiration. Steven King tells of when he was first starting, how he found a tiny back laundry-room space in his small living quarters where he wrote *Carrie*. Then again, what the hell kind of writing backstory would he have had to impart? He's not successful or anything.

I am all for getting out with the laptop, balancing it on your knees as you sit on a beach or some far-off mountain deck. But generally speaking; I think it's a good idea, if you can manage it, to have one place that, when you walk into it — be it backroom, shed, cramped attic alcove — is the place where, for the most part (and again this depends on how cramped your living space might be) you go to write. But hey, if you can indeed write on a beach or a far-off mountain deck with any regularity, my hats off to you.

Also, let's admit this, we're all adults here: if you happen to be penning erotica and what you write gets you all hot and bothered, and you feel you have to...do I have to spell the rest of this out for you? When a moment like this takes you, you'll want/need a little privacy.

2.) **Find the right tools.** If you enjoy clacking away on a manual typewriter, then get yourself one. I have a very good friend who collects them, another who happens to find them infinitely sexy; both write on them. I don't happen to use one, so I can't tell you what the availability of these machines is presently, but if this is your weapon of choice to slay the dragons of the literary world, then write on it. The point is, be it a #2 pencil and yellow lined paper (Woody Allen lays on his bed, scribbling out the first drafts of his movies with a pen and lined paper pads) or the old Intel processor HP laptop, choose what works for you and go forth.

Don't be resistant to changing your tools, though. When I first began working in Word, I recall telling my buddy, walking me through the process, that the idea of 'cutting and pasting' was something I was sure I'd never get used to. These days, I can't write any other way than in a word processing program. In fact, my producer and I use almost the very same technology in the studio when I am recording.

3.) **Set a schedule.** Again, not as easily done as considered, especially if writing is not (yet) your full-time gig. And I know as many writers who need the discipline (no, not the discipline of a paddle bounced across their backside...Jesus, get your mind out of the gutter!) of a set time to sit down and ply their wares as plenty more who function best just sitting down when the mood strikes. As my buddy and fantabulous scribe M. Christian will tell you, he and I think of ourselves as 'hacks,' in the very best sense of that word. We don't wait for the muse to whisper in our ear and only then get to writing. We tend to go to our writing space each morning and get on with the getting on, answering emails, attending to open assignments, looking for jobs, etc. But amateurs and pros can have a bunch of different ways of setting a schedule if they set one at all.

And even in setting one, a schedule can certainly change. A new baby in the house (you know how those darn babies are, they just drop in of the sky when you least expect them!), the time a new employer is open and operating (say you just scored a client who is clear across the world from you and you need to be up sometimes at odd hours to communicate with them) and plenty of other unforeseen life intrusions can spin one off a routine/schedule right quick. It's good to stay flexible in this regard.

4.) **Schedule time *not* to write.** This one is especially hard for me, as I find myself pretty much writing all the time. It's really what I like to do, as much as I can do it. As I've mentioned, Isaac Asimov used to say how his wife was always on him to take vacations, but he would repeatedly tell her he had no need for them. That's the way it is for me. With my writing I get to travel to a whole bunch of different places, meet a whole bunch of cool people, and indulge my perfectly muscled (and superbly hung) body in many ways. So why would I want to take time away from writing?

But as I've advised throughout here, we all need to take time not to write/work.

Nowadays, we are surely prompted less and less to get out and about, social media and Amazon deliveries making it all too easy to stay put. And that damned VID thing didn't help matters either. But as much as you need to push off from that keyboard and lift your ass from your desk, you need to go further and farther by taking a walk around the block every now and then, get in the car for a long drive, sit with friends over brunch, etc. Nothing brushes those old brain cobwebs away faster than to pluck yourself away from the work at hand and be out among the sunshine or rain.

5.) **Work to some sort of organization.** Lots of writers see the word 'organization' and go screaming off into the night. I understand. You should see my desk. Talk about a mess! But I have a manner of organization set, a method to my madness, a way of keeping track, as much on my desktop as in my mind (both cluttered spaces that are always in danger of losing their ever-dwindling power) that does work for me, when I work to work it. I certainly am not championing compulsive neatness here, nor do I think trying to order your space should take precedence over your writing. But if you can find a system that works for you, some way of alleviating the chaos, ease your mind a bit, take to it. You might run through a few trials and errors before you land on a way of righting your listing ship, but there's nothing wrong with making things a little easier on yourself.

I generally don't like anything mucking-up my mind — limited as it is — when I sit down to write. A pending phone call, or a roast in the oven, will lead me to distraction unless I take care of these things prior to sitting down. I am also constantly closing open word processing documents, even if I am not yet done with them, but I know I have to attend to something else presently. I just can't have lots of things open on my desktop. They can be there, sure, labeled under various folders, but I need to have only one document open at a time to do my best unless the work demands I shuttle between two open fields simultaneously. But, as I say, you need to find how best to organize, even if it is only you organizing the slightest bit.

I hope some of, or maybe even all of the above, will help you in your routine, if you need help with it. I am sure you have habits you adhere to that get you through your day, and yes, being writers of smut, we might be a little more quirky than other writers. Although, I dare say all writers are probably pretty quirky.

Hell, come to think of it, everybody's pretty awfully quirky in their own way, no?

12.
Step Back, Shut Up, F' Off!

In its original form, this was a plea column to playwrights, but I revised it here to include us all in making this chapter. What I am on about here falls well beyond the advice I gave about backing off a piece of writing, letting the thing you are creating just be, considering it done as opposed to picking at it, and editing it to death. In this chapter, I address a specific behavior *about* the work, the tiresome need writers/musicians/actors/so-called 'creatives' have to yawp too much about what they do, have just done, or might be presently giving themselves forth into, upward and on.

You see this played out too many times when a singer/songwriter sits down to play a song but spends more time talking about the song's inspiration than they do playing it. You'll get it all too often when you ask an actor about their latest performance, and they all too quickly rifle off their resume and past critics' notices. Ask a writer about his or her latest book, and they are all too happy to tell you about the lives of their fictional characters. Plenty more people will give out the specifics of their websites, Facebook page, Instagram, or Twitter handle well before you even ask for it. To me, this kind of self-promotion/white noise drips of desperation, kind of like how the populace seems to have an addiction to posting every idea, vacation pic, and political rant.

Shit, don't get me started on the epidemic of narcissism birthed by social media.

I understand we who create stuff and get it out there (and, as I have been writing here all along, everybody creates stuff, all of us are artists in some sense, so I don't hold musicians, actors, writers, etc. in higher regard than anybody else) feel we need to consistently show ourselves, be seen and heard above everybody else trying to be seen and heard. I understand that there comes more rejection than ever acceptance, when making stuff. But one comes from an infinitely stronger base, reveals the confidence of one's convictions, and surely the strength of their work, when one just does the thing and doesn't talk about the thing unless one is asked to speak about the thing by people who want to hear about how one did or does the thing, or are paying for one to talk about all that doing.

Let me tell you a story ("Jeez Ralph, another one?!" I hear you scream) that will tie this all up neatly in a bow. Going back to my play-making and what this chapter initially sprang from…

I have found infinite pleasure writing for the stage, not only because I get to hear my words spoken out loud but because I get to work with actors, directors, and crews, a kind of collaboration I don't find when I usually write something. And quite a few times in the community theatres that have 'put up' my plays, there's been a Q&A after the performance, where audiences are invited to ask questions of directors, actors, and writers. For a writer especially, this public airing can be both fun and unnerving.

We get to come out into the light beyond our garrett and react to actual human beings, but at the same time, that light can be blinding when somebody starts asking you about what you meant by this or that when you might not have a clear or even a wise-ass answer. Luckily, from my performance background, especially playing music for kids — the toughest audiences you are ever likely to meet — I am pretty quick on my toes and mostly lead with self-effacing humor, which diffuses even the most serious, personal queries. So, although I am asked to talk about me and the work, I try to keep it light, not get so bogged down in my "process," and entertain with my answers.

I have also enjoyed the singular honor of being invited to attend a rehearsal of one of my plays. This is rarefied time for a writer, and I feel they should treat it as such. Taking to this invite, I had the good sense to sit quietly with the director during the time it took the actors to run through the action and dialogue, jotting notes down secretly in my notebook at my side. Post the run-thru, the two actors, the director, and I had a sit-down and it was only then that I began to give forth my thoughts, prompted as I was by the small group.

Still, I 'stayed in my lane' only talking about how I thought *I* could make the play better by excising some of what *I* wrote. It was not my place to critique acting performances or the director's ideas, not that I would ever dream of doing so, know nothing about such things and was not asked for this kind of opinion. But not to make too large a point on this, and surely why playwrights are typically not invited to rehearsals, it is well known how too many a playwright walk into a *the-ate-er,* feeling their words are ever so sacrosanct. Playwrights typically never concede any point when it comes to their words and walk around as if anyone who even dare questions a line is not being respectful to the work.

You can guess how I feel this kind of a superior attitude some writers, a lot of creative types take, is a load of b.s.

I guess the director sensed from meeting me prior to the rehearsal that I was not this way and figured I'd be safe to invite along. This made me feel great, as much because I got to spy the play before it 'went up' as the fact that I gave off what was most certainly the humble attitude I certainly feel in situations where somebody wants to work with little ol me.

I also came to realize something I had assumed all the while…a good actor can convey as much or even more with a facial expression, body movement or a director with smart blocking than I ever can with a witty turn of phrase. If the omission of a line or two can make actors flow their way across my dialogue/the action/their performance easier, I am all too willing to make changes, which I did in this instance. I could see the relief cross the two actors' faces as they regarded the particular lines I wanted to cut as clunky as they did. I even cut more dialogue when I realized the actors were getting more across in how they moved, how they chewed a line or let it go, even their distance from one another (the director's 'blocking') basically *showing* better in this case than *telling*. In this instance, it wasn't so much a case of me, the writer, shutting up, stepping back, or f-ing off, as much as it was simply excising the words I wrote.

Whether answering an audience's post-show wrap-up Q&A, speaking to a writing class, penning advice on the website that ran some of these columns and was the basis of this book, or meeting with and talking to actors and directors working with my script or even in writing this book, if somebody has come to seek/read/look for my advice, asks for or wants to read my opinion, I'm willing and humbled to give what I know. But generally speaking, I try to step back, shut up, and fuck off about this writing thing. I keep out of the way of other people's creativity unless they ask me to come along, and even then, my go-to is to demure. And when I come upon somebody reciting their resume of the many books they have published with this or that publisher, I nod and compliment them on their good fortune but feel no compulsion to compete.

I can't express this enough, and again I don't care if you are a writer, candlestick-maker, or chef, really, sometimes — strike that, *most times* — you are better off doing what the title of this chapter suggests.

13.

Write What You Know?

Okay, confession time. Not everything I write falls into that 'Write What You Know' category, especially with my erotica. I'd either have to be very lucky or, by extension, exceedingly exhausted to have done all of what I write. My favorite writer, Ray Bradbury, certainly someone who had never been to the planet Mars, still so elegantly wrote about the place in his seminal *The Martian Chronicles* (if you have never read it, I urge you to, right now, go ahead…really….I'll wait). He said of his imaginative traveling: "I came on the old and best ways of writing through ignorance and experiment and was startled when truths leaped out of brushes like quail before gunshot."

Ray B. merely worked hard to dream where he wanted to go and then went there.

As any adult with a few relationships under their belt can relate, it's sometimes best to keep a fantasy strictly fantasy. The third person in your *ménage à* tickle might turn out to be a lot clingier than you and your regular partner want them to be; the chocolate sauce really gets very sticky when…well, you get the idea. Things birthed within our fevered imaginings don't always the best reality make, but they sometimes do provide the goods for good stories. In fact, a case could be made that those things you do not make real, have never experienced, might make for the best fiction as they have always been fiction to you anyway.

Surely, it's best to go forth with at least a modicum of facts about the action at hand, even if it is something you've never tried, and one of the main reasons that 'write what you know' axiom is so often advised. For example, a criticism I repeatedly heard about E.L. James' *Fifty Shades of Gray* came from kinksters who said that the primary power-play relationship portrayed in the books felt false. And although this is a subjective assessment of the trilogy, authenticity *is* essential when writing about trussing your lover to an overhead beam as much as figuring out the best propulsion to use, and how to use it, in a rocket ship.

Conversely, layering details doesn't always make for a spectacular read. I recall trying to slog through the one thousand pages Anne Rice set herself midway through her otherwise engaging *The Witching Hour*. Relating the history of her Talamasca sect, Rice offered a rich background, but for me, the book ground to a halt with such a detailed history. Who am I to criticize Anne Rice, the lady was a smashingly fantastic fantasist and a lovely person (I met her at a book signing once, and she actually called me "darling"). But have you a penchant for giving forth on what every whip crack feels like as it bounces off a sub's skin or what the air on a particular planet smells like, remember, details are only useful for however long you can maintain their effectiveness. You also don't want to come across as a smartie pants. Sure, this is your journey, but —

(And just as an aside. I have to tell you, I hate that word, 'journey.' It's like when I hear someone who create something call the work their "process." Good God, what you made wasn't as difficult as rocket science or brain surgery! I mean, I like the word Journey well enough....and the band even. Still, every time I see some actor describing a character or semi-celeb reality star talking about his or her 'journey,' or the 'process' of working a creation into being, I feel the bile rise. Sorry, as I was saying...)

— all too often in erotica, I find authors get too mired in the minutia as if they are trying to impress upon me all the wild sex they have engaged in and how well they know stuff. Yeah, yeah, I get it, you are super peachy-cool, wild-in-bed, and conversant in all the many ways to tie a knot, but is the tale you are relaying interesting? Does it move me emotionally? Might you not be getting too bogged down trying to impress me with all your knowledge?

This writing thing is a balance of imparting what you have experienced, what you dream about, your skills at embellishment, and infusing your fiction with "truths leaping(sic) out of brushes like quail before gunshot," as Ray B. tells us (see the beginning of this chapter). Write what you know, what you imagine, what you wish, but mostly, what *you* want to read best that you can.

Chances are, *I* might want to read it as well.

14.
Writing Dirty For Slightly Alternative Markets

Mainly, so far, I have concentrated here on fiction and article writing. But I'd be remiss if I didn't explore the plenty of other kinds of sweetly salacious writing you can manage: interviews, playwriting, poems, songwriting, web copy, captions, toy reviews and descriptions, scripts and advertisements, movie blurbs, adds, teleplays, comics and emails, and press releases, to name but a few.

Adult toy descriptions, web copy, captions, advertisements, and press releases almost all have strict parameters set. It's been my experience that press releases, be they for the mainstream space or adult, tend towards following the current A.P. style (be careful, though, this style changes its rules all the time). In most of the modern-day descriptions of adult toys that I have written, and I write plenty, (one of the perks here is that you usually get the toy sent to you so you can properly "review it," such is the arduous world of the researcher) I am given specific keywords that the client wants to see in the copy, with the density percentage of those words set. These descriptions usually balance a 'how to' kind-of-a-thing, allowing lots of space to stuff in as many keywords as desired, with what's called "call to action" words to get readers to click and buy the item.

The most creative job I had in this particular field was when I was hired to write short, short fiction that featured a specific product the client wanted to highlight for a particular week. That certainly lifted the usual dry writing of just describing what the toy was, what it did, and its specific features into slightly more entertaining copy. I have only come across one toy maker/distributor who tried this approach but have often thought describing the toys through fiction would work for so many other sites that might want to present something to shoppers other than the usual nuts-and-bolts, keyword-stuffed copy.

Whether on Skype or Zoom, in-person, on the phone, or via some well-considered email questions, I have managed to land and write many adult-based interviews. Sitting across the subject in person, on the phone, even from sending email questions, as old Judge Judy is fond of saying, a writer needs to use their two ears ever much more than they ever do their one mouth, listening to record the words of their subject more than they ever should be talking.

The fun for me mostly comes after the meet-up or in receiving the answers to my questions when I have to fashion the interview into an easy ebb-and-flow of questions to answers and provide the reader a good overall insight into the person I interviewed. And while this kind of writing really is mostly an ad/promotion for the subject, the trick here is in making the interview not seem to be.

Although I did partner with another naughty writer/publicist/friend to pen a T.V. series bible/pilot script/character breakdown, this is as far as I have ever traveled in developing/writing a treatment or anything that could be considered a teleplay or screenplay. With the story pretty damn naughty and full of substance, my buddy and I felt we had enough fodder for a few season's run (at least) and managed to scare up some actual interest from a network show producer (who my buddy knew) and a series 'runner.' What we never counted on was that there were lots of other writers and producers (even one major Hollywood action star) who had very similar show ideas in development. Being nobodies in the Hollywood production game, we were left in the dust, but we later found out that all we had heard about being developed never saw fruition as is the case of so much writing hoping to make it to the small or big screen. But along the way, even if a show isn't produced or aired, plenty of times, writers are at least paid for their work, and they make headway into other projects even when one is denied them.

At the very least, my buddy and I were hoping for this entrée.

I mentioned emails above, and I did, for a time, manage and write email correspondence for an escort. This was interesting work, to say the least, responding to her clients in her voice with what she didn't have the time to write herself. As I mentioned before, I have also written scripts for short scenes, pre-recorded phone lines, not so much in vogue any longer, and naughty comics, but since I don't draw, I have always been paired with an illustrator. This can be challenging, honing scenes with your words that rely mainly on the visual.

You'll likely have the most creative leeway in songs, poems, and playwriting. But it should come as no surprise this is where you stand to make the least money unless you get exceedingly lucky, are in the right place at the right time, or just 'have a hit.' I have written whole shows centered around naughty songs, have even had them produced off-off-off Broadway, and have taken to writing quite a few one-acts (the only kind of playwriting I do actually) that have had some salaciously fun material as their base. A step-up from limerick writing, which I believe is a skill in and of itself, I have also managed to pen quite a few dirty poems.

And, of course, you can teach naughty writing. Hell, you can even write a book about it.

What I am on about here is that there are plenty of other ways to engage your lusts, fingers, and brain with writing that might not just be just fiction or a "How-To Peg You Man" blog. And speaking of pegging, I hope some of my above suggestions 'fit' you.

15.
Writing Naughty Dialogue

What somebody says can be just as interesting and downright wonderfully perverted as what they do. Or so I try to write in my fiction. Sure, there are those scenes where I have two or more people baring their pink parts for various tickles, touches, and teasing, save a moan or two, in complete silence. But lots of times, my characters talk a good bunch of the naughty before they get down, especially when one character is domming another and might want to mentally tease and taunt a sub well before they do so physically. So, writing naughty dialogue is very important in my view.

How do you do it then?

Hell if I know...

Ok, this is not true. I do know. But as with everything else I have imparted here, how you write a few lines of back-and-forth banter or a long single-character diatribe should come from your unique take on how you come to write a scene and how you believe your characters should sound. Sure, there are those instances where somebody might be enacting a little role-play and speak in a manner they usually don't: baby talk, stern master or mistress promises, even maybe with an accent they don't have. But, as you do with all of your erotica, you should be searching for truth in your words, be they dialogue or description. When a character opens their mouth, they should sound like how you have established them to be along the way unless they are possessed, schizophrenic, undergoing some sure stress, or, again, playing a role.

Now, beyond what you have one person say to or because of another, there is also *how* you foray forth their speaking.

Steven King offers a caution in his book *On Writing: A Memoir of the Craft* about the oft-used 'he said,' 'she moaned,' 'he admitted,' dialogue descriptors. He does have a point. That extra stuff added at the end of each line of snappy banter or a red-hot seduction scene could very well slow things down. And I agree with Mr. King where he says that once you have established who is speaking to whom, you can probably let go of the 'he/she said' stuff unless a character is doing something specific when speaking that you want your audience to know.

"So, you admit you've been a bad boy," Juanita said, giving Tom's tight testicles another flick with her belt. You know, that kind of a thing.

I have managed whole pages of just dialogue, nothing else. But, I am also fond of letting loose with a "SMACK" or a "TITPAT" to describe the sounds a paddle makes on a pair of bare buttocks or just the drumming of fingers across the inside of a thigh. So, you might want to create dialogue as much from the words spoken as the sounds you want to relate, and as we all know, erotica offers many options for sound.

I have also read where writers create fantastic and often hysterical inner monologues for characters that read as if the character is speaking to another person or in an instance when a character is indeed speaking out loud but only to him or herself. I am a great one for talking to myself; it's when you start arguing with yourself that you have to start to worry. So, my characters have a lot to say to themselves, and sometimes they do so aloud.

As with all that we do in our daily scribbling, there is not just one way to bring this all off, as there is not just one reason you might come to write a dialogue passage.

*To get a leg up on great dialogue writing, you might want to seek out master sci-fi/fantastic Roger Zelazny. Zelazny has a masterful ability for writing dialogue so economically but at the same time so chock-full of a character's 'voice.' I refer you to his infamous *Amber Chronicles* for a master class on dialogue writing. Hell, read the *Amber Chronicles* anyway, they are just so so good.

We should all toil to be even a smidgen as good as Zelazny.*

Beyond King's warning of the, 'he said,' 'she explained,' markers, there are some other sure dialogue petards you could find yourself swinging from if you are not careful.

1.) **The dreaded 'info dump.'** It's all too easy, and all writers are probably guilty of this at least once in their story-making, to have a character deliver a whole bunch of facts, give a long and florid exposition, basically further the story by saying exactly what has happened, what might be happening, and what might happen. This urge to just dump information — the technical word is *exposition* — is something you must be careful not to slip into when writing dialogue.

2.) **The over-descriptive speaker.** If one character is in love with another, it is perfectly understandable that they might gush and fawn using lovey-dovey descriptors or ebullient praise on the object of their affection. But generally speaking people don't talk like this, and if they do, wouldn't you rather not be around them? All too often, a writer thinks that they can slip in a goodly amount of a character's physical characteristics by writing someone opposite of them fawning over their physical traits, as in, "Oh Gene, your blue eyes sparkle so wonderfully in your unlined long face." But it makes for bad exposition and just bad dialogue-ing.

3.) Following this, I have also seen, and probably managed to fall into this trap a time or two myself, writers **attempting to heat up a sex scene by having one person react or describe another's physical characteristics as they relate to that person sexually.** As in a "Oh Gene, you really are as thick as Jane said, your cock is stretching out my…" kind of a thing.

Man, this Gene guy is really something, huh?

4.) Your character simply **speaks too much.** I have written whole pages of just dialogue, as mentioned, even entire short stories of only the back-and-forth spoken lines between two people. But I always try to keep sentences clipped, the banter bouncy, the characters working off each following line as much as making their points. I once saw actor Oliver Platt in the play *Shining City* deliver what might have been one of the longest stage monologues I have ever heard live, smack dab in the middle of a scene where he was talking to and playing off two other characters. To keep a live audience invested and two other characters from not appearing as just stunned recipients of drawn-out drivel takes masterful writing, acting, and directing.

Want to try it in your writing? Tread lightly, I say.

Remember, nobody is forcing you to write dialogue, as much as nobody is telling you not to. This is your baby, your 'Journey' so "Don't Stop Believing!" Birth and nurture your scribbling the way you see fit. I'm just advising that if you feel some dialogue is suitable for a particular story, stay true to the characters, try and listen to how they speak (often reading dialogue aloud helps determine its authenticity in your ears), and don't get stuck on the idea of having to hold your reader's hand every step of the way with who is saying what when (as much as what they are saying). Also, stay well clear of the info dump and be confident in the fact that you can go for pages without any dialogue and still others where that's all there might be.

16.
Publishing Erotica: The Cold Hard Facts

Have you explored the present traditional publishing game? Where, years ago, you'd have one editor shepherding your book through the process of getting it to print (like A&R men of old helping to build a music act at a record label). Now, if you are lucky enough to get your manuscript seen at a publisher, even a small one, decisions on your work will be made by a team involved more in social media marketing concerns (as in how many Twitter follows might you have gathered before completing your book) than much of anything substantive.

And forget trying to find an agent, most are stuck in that Catch-22 loop of not mustering much interest in a writer unless that writer is well known enough from what they have published or across social media, when most writers can't enjoy this kind of popularity or attention unless they can score an agent who will land them a book deal or enough work to grow their social media swirl.

And even if you manage to get your foot (your book more precisely) into a publisher and then the much-coveted contract with them, your future isn't set. Do you know that presently in our scaredy-cat culture there are penalties presently worked into contracts where just about anyone from your publisher's team can terminate you if you commit what the publisher considers a breach of *moral turpitude*. Go ahead, look the term up, and see if you can even determine what it means, let alone how anybody could give an author enough of a definitive definition so they could understand if, or when, they commit this act. I absolutely shite you not that this clause exists in many a modern book contract (not the one I signed for this book though, super peachy cool the publisher of this book is). So, watch what you say to your Twitter followers or to the folks at your publisher.

So, what do you do, lowly unpublished erotica writer, penning stories where big globs of electrically infused jelly-like masses are doing nasty things to other electrically infused jelly-like masses? Is some publisher going to come along and agree to put out a book of your very odd, extremely niche content when bookstores are already running away from stuff that doesn't come with a historic healthy selling track record?

Don't worry. I'm here to help.

Let's start with…

SELF-PUBLISHING

I had the occasion and great honor to interview author S. Rodman, a successful self-published author of gay male paranormal romance books. He's done very well with self-publishing his naughty niche books, so I thought starting with his take on the world of self-publishing would undoubtedly get us all up to speed and maybe prompt you to go this route. I have no dog in the fight here with which way you go, save saving you from a vanity press.

More on them later.

Here is my interview with S. Rodman:

You obviously have had success self-publishing. If you could give one overall word or piece of advice for writers looking to proceed this way, what would it be? (And it could certainly be more than one tidbit, of course).

Covers and titles are your keys to success. When customers are browsing for books, the cover and title are the only things they have to go on. The cover needs to fit your genre, and your title needs to be clear. For example, 'Crimson Dawn' versus 'Ride On: A Gay Western Romance'? Which tells readers what you are offering?

Blurbs are also very important. Getting your keywords right is essential. There is a ton of information and resources out there. Be prepared to spend a lot of time learning.

Being successful in self-publishing is 20% writing the book and 80% learning how to enable customers to see it. It's a business, and you need to think of it as such.

I assume making your presence known on social media is key to making a successful run at self-publishing. But how does one know what portals or pursuits to spend their time on when there is so much out there these days to post, tweet and twat over?

Actually, not so much *(*man, was I ever heartened to hear this!*)* When people are on social media, they are not looking for a book to buy. Sure, they may see yours and like the look of it, but it's well known in marketing that online a person's attention span is only around three seconds. Holding it long enough to get them to click through to Amazon and buy your book is super tough.

Amazon is full of customers actively looking for a book to buy. And if we go back to my title example, some are actually looking for a gay western romance right now. It is far more productive to spend your time ensuring that they see your book. Shouting into the internet void and hoping to find someone who this very instant is looking for gay western romance is not very productive.

Going the self-publishing route, how did you cobble together a book designer, copyrighting, etc.? How does one vet these various professionals?

Word of mouth. That is what social media is great for, finding fellow authors in your genre. And I stress the 'in your genre' part is super important. Erotica writers' needs have little in common with authors of military history.

No matter how hard you pursue it, what won't you ever get from self-publishing?

The only thing I can think of is…respect. The world has changed, but there are still an awful lot of people who think self-publishing is the realm of sad, vain losers who can't accept that they are not good enough to be published. Truthfully, I thought that a year ago that people will never respect you as an author because they believe you 'aren't really published.'

Following…assuming there are advantages, what would you say are the biggest reasons to self-publish?

Not to be shallow, but money. I know plenty of self-published authors who are making a comfortable living and a few who are on six figures. Most trad. published authors, even NYT (S. Rodman is abbreviating for the *New York Times'* best seller book list here) bestsellers, make $6,000 a year. Go on, go Google it.

What does a writer of erotica need to be leery of when self-publishing?

1. There are far more people making huge amounts of money 'helping' people to self-publish than there are people actually making money from self-publishing. Don't fall sway to these people. There are a ton of free resources out there. Do the free taster sessions but don't sign up to the paid stuff. It's often not worth it (*more on this later*).

2. Don't think you can just click submit on your book and sit back. Submitting your book to Amazon puts it in the virtual stockroom. You need to make sure it actually gets on the shelves.

That's where your title, cover, blurb, keywords, and categories come in. You get those right, and you are away.

Would you still court or want to try and find a trad. publisher for anything you have coming up?

I was trad. published. That's how I started. I left trad. publishing for self-publishing, much to my publisher's dismay. I would never go back. I made 10% of what I am making now, and now I can scale up, which just never would have happened with trad.

All trade publishers do for you is pay for editing, formatting, a cover, and a tiny bit of marketing. What they take back in their cut far exceeds the price of these things. In my honest opinion, in this modern day and age, trad. publishers are obsolete. An unnecessary middleman. Especially for erotica, there are extraordinarily few trad. authors doing well in erotica. It really is the playground of the self-published.

And publishers are slow, behind the times. Unable to keep up with trends and marketing techniques.

Taking the whole book market, not just erotica. 98% of trad published books sell fewer than 5,000 copies in their lifetime. It's a myth that trade is the key to success. Even if you hate the idea of marketing - trad. publishers expect authors to do the lion's share of it.

Yes, really!

So, no, I will never try trad publishing again.

Find S. Rodman's work here: S. Rodman MM romance author (srodman.net)

VANITY PRESS

Feeling good about the DIY route after reading the above? Well, you can and should.

S. Rodman is right. With a little research, and some referrals, you can find copywriters, layout people, cover artists, P.R. (press release) writers, and marketers all on your own. You do not have to pay someone to help you round up these folks. Or pay a supposed publisher who is nothing more than a contractor. There are plenty of these companies out there, pretty much pressing on your vanity.

(See how I did that just now, introducing my section here about vanity presses, I used the words "pressing on your vanity." And this far in, you didn't think you could be amazed any further at my way with words, huh?)

Vanity presses lie in wait for novice authors, exploiting newbies — and even some dyed-in-the-wool writers who should know better, like me — pushing that big button of "respect" that Rodman mentions above, well-aware how most writers have a genuine mental hard-on on wanting to have somebody, anybody, publish their book.

Of course, in the language of their contracts, the vanity press (sometimes called a "subsidiary press") covers their asses by calling all their services "invaluable," promising that their accounting department will stay on top of all the money your book makes from its sales, assuring the uninitiated that their royalty rate is "generous," and that in no time, even with a/the split on the sales you make through them (with the percentage always leaning in their favor) you'll see a return on your investment enjoying the full and far-reaching influence of their well-oiled distribution network.

I know, take a breath, that was a long one sentence paragraph of negatives, but believe me, it's all true.

This bears emphasizing: **the vanity press bleeds a payment from you at the start, then they still take a percentage of your sales as long as they have your title. So, in effect, they are double-dipping, worse than anything you ever saw perpetrated on** *Seinfeld.*

Most vanity presses, though, allow authors entering into their crock-of-shitter-y deal the ability to pay off the requisite upfront fees in installments.

How nice of them.

I have had a few run-ins with these particular kinds of crooks. Once, when I was a fledgling writer and didn't know any better, I only got about a third of the way into their net before I sensed something fishy and pulled away. Fast forward, though, to just recently, and I was drawn in again, from a very slick and seemingly pro-publishing outfit, when sending out one of my children's books. Within a week of uploading the book to their portal, I was sent a rather complimentary long email about how the company higher-ups had loved the book, but given my lack of credits in getting a kid's book to bookstore shelves save for the efforts my illustrator/half creator buddy and I have managed so far in self-publishing 16 titles in four years, this publisher couldn't see spending time, money and resources on what they considered a risky endeavor. We weren't risky enough though, because this publisher did offer to split the costs of the book's production and marketing with me. And you guessed it, they wanted money upfront to do so.

HYBRID PUBLISHING

Just to make things even more confusing, there's also something called "hybrid publishing," a broad term used in many different ways. In general, it refers to a publishing house where, again, the author pays for all services up front but is allowed a more significant cut of the royalties of book sales. Usually, a hybrid publisher has a modicum (very small, but they exist) of standards and will not just publish every book that they see. Still, you have to be careful here, as you'll be charged an f-load for services and the distribution network of these places is sketchy at best. These kinds of companies are only one step up from a vanity press.

"Amazon Me, Bitch!"

Of course, sooner than later, you will trip over or maybe even fall into the Amazon rabbit hole. As you read from what S Rodman said, and pretty much as you'll know from everybody you hear always asking the same question," Is your book on Amazon?" every product, be it a book, toaster, or dildo (which is the name of my most favorite country band: "Ladies and Gentleman, please welcome, Book/Toaster/Dildo!") ends up on the online retail portal. And as you well know, pretty much, you're not thought of having anything worth buying if you're not selling your whatever-it-is on Amazon. But whether your book ends up there from your efforts or via your publisher posting it on the big A, here are a few facts about the online giant:

1.) **Anybody can publish on Amazon.** The formatting is relatively easy to negotiate, and Amazon has plenty of tutorials on how to get your book up with them. If you are paying someone to put your book up on Amazon you might want to think twice and do this yourself.

2.) **Amazon is still sketchy when it comes to erotica.** I have mentioned this in other columns, in books, and my classes. Amazon can/will and has determined that when it comes to erotica, they move the goal posts at whim over just what subjects, even what words, they'll allow at any given time. Subjects like age-play, certainly anything that has to do with kinks between people even *pretending* to be family members (this includes characters calling each other "mommy" or "naughty baby boy" in a story), get red flagged by Amazon all the time. I wish I could alert you to their present policy, but as I say, the portal is forever changing its mind.

3.) A trick many Amazon authors either know well or come to find out is that, **once your book is uploaded, you can, in most instances,**

order an author's copy for less than it normally costs to buy the book. So then, not only do you get to have a hot little copy of your book in your equally smoldering little hands, but you can use this as a "gallery proof" that you can scrutinize for any changes you still might want to make. I don't know about you, but I happen to be of the old school where I can make better editing choices holding a printed manuscript in my hands than reading that same manuscript from a computer screen. And without the headache of printing a box full of books only to realize later changes still need to be made — something that has surely happened to me more than once — snatching one copy from Amazon for a last look-see as much as for a possible revision, you only pay for one book.

But be cautioned and pay attention, especially here, to my point #1. Like all else we find on the net these days, there is a glut of stuff out there, and not so much of it, well, good. Sure, that's a subjective distinction, I know, but with the template easy to negotiate and everybody pretty much thinking they have a story worth telling that somebody will want to read, you can bet there is a wide variety of 'quality' available to readers online. And I get shit for saying this all the time, but no, the cream does not rise to the top. Audience supply and demand has not, nor will it ever, level the playing field. More often, in all present areas of life, admitted or not, the mediocre middle is what becomes popular. How could it not? The net is the driver here, and the net is the depository (and I can all too easily substitute the word suppository for depository when talking about all the crap you can find online) of the mundane, the uninteresting, those who speak loudest and post most often but have very little of real substance to offer. Yes, I am an elitist snob, but you know what I say here is true.

Remember, your book, up on Amazon, or any other online book listing, via your efforts, or via your publisher, is just one of many. Then again, you read how well S. Rodman is doing.

THE OLD HUMP & HAWK

I know what I impart in this section works because I have and continue to do it. Find a local bookstore in the area, or some other place that kinda/maybe sells stuff that is in the ballpark of what your book is about, stop in, talk to the owner or manager and see if you might plop your book on their self on consignment. Lots of smaller/local bookstores do this, even some of the bigger ones, with the store usually managing a 30%/70% book sale split, in your favor. These smaller spots even support author events and signings or some other kind of in-store marketing.

As I say, I have done and do just what I describe above, often with my children's titles. But securing a consignment doesn't have to necessarily be only for a children's bookstore. Sure, my illustrator and I have gone into a few, did some readings and signings, or participated in a book fair connected with the store. But we have also set up meet-and-greets during Christmas time at a few art supply brick-and-mortars. There were enough families coming through, especially at that time of year, that these matches worked out pretty good for us.

For erotica, you'd be surprised how an adult toy store (yeah, you've seen them when driving around, don't lie), a lingerie boutique or even a cool vinyl record shop might be interested in partnering with you.

You are not going to make a ton of money this way. First of all, you have to pay to print copies of your book so you can leave a few on the store's shelf, have one or two to hand out gratis, or for sale at your in-store signing. And how well your book sells in consignment is as much up to you and your possible appearances and social media reach as it is how well the bookstore promotes it. But you might be able to get the word out, sell a few copies, and considering how far you are willing to drive, you might very well get to drop your tome at some cool places maybe a few miles from your 'burb.

So get out, be happy, have some books ready to drop off and sell yourself.

SMALLER INDEPENDENT PRESSES

Here's where I can speak with some authority.

All my adult books, adult, sci-fi, as well a few of the ones I have written for children, have been released via smaller independent presses. Be they publishers in the U.S. or abroad, strictly eBook houses, selling only niche content or many different kinds of books, what I have found and continue to find with these smaller houses is a commitment from the folks who run these businesses (and so far I have always dealt directly with the person who runs the house) to do their best for their authors, to get a whole bunch of titles up and out, to work so damn hard on each book and to, very often, beat the hell out of larger houses with their singular passion.

A win-win all around.

I value the one-on-one intimacy born from working with someone who has my best interests at heart and who cares who they add to their stable of authors. Someone, who I know I can pretty much get on the phone or across email with quickly, who cares about my input, who will work with me when we both don't know the answer to a question to try and find the best solution. Sure, there is little to no money upfront when signing with a small independent press — usually the folks who run these houses have just enough for a small marketing budget, to create a website and maybe set up a POD (print on demand) portal — but I also know for a fact that too many authors who sign with a big publishing company never see a dime from book sales, as any money they are given up front gets gobbled up from sales paid back to the publisher since almost always advances are recuperable (I know this for a fact, in fact).

You read what S. Rodman had to say on this subject and he is right! And don't get me started on the horror stories I have heard where writers and illustrators lose most, if not all, artistic control when signing with a big company who claims to know how to *do* the book better.

With distribution now up for grabs, anyone can, and plenty people do, jump into the many different ways to make a solid living where they retain more of their rights and their vision isn't compromised by either partnering with an independent publisher, or allowing for maybe a one-book run to test the waters with someone local who works their ass off for a product they really believe in. And sure, there are charlatans and sharks out there in the small press world, and sometimes due to smaller budgets they have to stick to one kind of book or maybe only align with authors from the same geographical region. But from my experience, with a great many of them, I say, give me a smaller, independent press, any day.

So, in the end, what should you do?

Sorry, that's for you to decide. But tread lightly. Do as much deep dive research of the publisher who says they want you, as much the person who designs your jacket's cover as how to get your book seen and bought on the big A. Network, find others who write the stuff you do, and talk to them about how they got around to getting their book to the masses. Or plop a few copies of your latest spanking story collection into the backseat of your ride and go out looking into the wild blue yonder for a sympathetic bookstore and maybe an 'adult boutique' you have GPS-ed.

One thing is for certain — there are lots of ways these days to get a book into the hands of readers.

17.

Marketing or Can A Writer Be Too Social These Days?

What I admit here, I know, will instantly stain me with pariah status: I am not 'on' any social media platforms. I am not a Facebooker. I do not tweet or twat, Snapchat, or post to Instagram. I even try to censor how much I text. Yes, I am better than you because of this, more evolved, just that much cooler. I'm joking. Actually, I make no judgments about how you come to spend your time, as I do not want you judging me on how I spend mine. Do whatever you like when it comes to social media-ing; just don't assume I am 'on,' have read one of your posts, or know much, if anything at all, about who is doing what on TikTok.

Sure, I know I truncate my job prospects by not being social in the digital sphere. I see plenty of job postings asking for writers to help with social media feeds or just for the applicant to give their LinkedIn info. I know many authors who spend time chasing reviews, working their Twitter networks day and night. I have seen Substack and other newsletters and realize their potential effectiveness. But all this noise doesn't interest me. While I understand how and why it all works, when it does, and I am often called upon to write click-worthy SEO copy, I leave all the real social media writing work and online connecting for those who know how to do it and, furthermore, want to.

Call me a Neo-Luddite, accuse me of cutting off my nose to spite my face, berate me over why I am not more successful. But I took this stance a long time ago, and it's the way I wish to conduct my life and business. As I always say, and should be apparent from what you have read thus far here: you do you, I'll do me.

But what I will conjecture about all this social media-ing for those embroiled in it is that you are probably dealing with the double-edged sword I have noticed plenty of my fellow savvy scribes try not to get cut with. As my buddy and fellow smut writer M. Christian says all the time, he's consistently balancing his social media-ing with time to write. One can all too easily spend many an hour chasing tweets, posting, and staying on one's phone to all hours being 'social.' But I dare think, if you write for a living, you need to have some writing from which to make your living, and the more time you spend twirling your giblets around social media, the less time you get to write.

To let us all off the hook a smidgen, as science explains, being as enraptured with social media as we are might not be something we can rightly ignore. According to the big-brain guys and girls of this world, the old, dumb mammals that we are, receive an actual Dopamine surge when we hear a "Weewho," feel our phone vibrate, promoting a new 'like.' It's akin to the same shot of chemicals that rush through our pleasure center when we sit at a slot machine: lights go off, colors swirl, bells chime and we are caught. Despite what a time-suck, mind-numbing narcotic it might be — and we all realize it is — because of the way our brains work, we just might not have the wherewithal to avoid the prompts, buzzes, and pretty lights and feel actual anxiety when we don't reply to a tweet or text.

My other caution here is that there is such a great glut of stuff out there — writings, music, political ramblings, videos — it's much harder to be heard or noticed above that din. You must ask yourself: Do I want to be part of all of that? And in becoming part of all that, will I indeed be lending my voice in some substantive manner to the wave, or simply drown under it?

I have had first-hand experience seeing someone spend hours and precious coin on social media, which never saw any substantive results. For a good three years, the CEO of a magazine and website I was editor-in-chief for chased various well-known online depositories/suppositories, hoping to make a mark with what I thought was a unique publication. He spent untold thousands, and we made no real inroads, at least none that were worth the money and time spent. I know plenty of bands and musicians who list their gigs on Facebook and still draw no audience. And I have a partner involved with me in a specific publishing concern who fights me all the time — not in fisticuffs, more good-natured arguments — over the importance of posting on Instagram and building a stronger online presence. But I'm sure you can show me a band that is building a substantial following across their social media postings, a star who is making millions only from ever posting on TikTok. And sure, plenty of writers are pulling in hundreds of weekly self-publishing on Amazon (you read my interview with S. Rodman in the last chapter, right?) and advertising via a newsletter they email their followers weekly.

I keep thinking all of this modern social connecting will reach a critical mass end point (if it hasn't already), and as we always seemed to, the culture will retreat, taking their collective interest in another direction all too soon. But this need to be heard (more than ever a need to listen) is epidemic in modern society and seems to be increasing in its severity (and yes, I hinted at this before, I know). Have you read what passes for news these days — real, fake, or otherwise — and how quickly great big gobs of the population are all too ready to believe what they read and then change their mind when they read something else the next day, hour, minute? This is the climate in which we are all trying to advertise our wares. While the general consensus is that since the creator of the thing has nearly ultimate control now, it is better for the creator and their audience, there are, to my mind, way too many cooks in the proverbial kitchen, and the damn stove just isn't big enough.

Or it's used too often that we all risk getting burned more than we ever might cook anything that is going to taste good.

Yes, enough with the metaphors already, I know. But you get my meaning here, right? Embroiling yourself in social media can make Jack or Jill a very dull boy/girl/or both, indeed. And if you want to play in this sandbox and get more than just sand from it, these days, you are going to well have to think out of and around that box best you can.

18.

De-balling, Retracting and Playing It Safe: How Cultural Inclusionary Language Is Killing Sex Writing or 'You Better Watch What You Write, You Dirty Writer You!'

Like lots of writers, I use the Grammarly program for my editing, but lately I have become ever so cautious of it. I notice that the algorithm has an annoying way of spitting back suggestions over my word choices that it feels may not be known by the general public or scolding me to use gender neutral words.

Go figure. My vocabulary is that highfalutin? And I'm looking to be exclusionary?

Grammarly has spanked me for using the word *salesman*, but what happens if the person I am writing about happens *to be* a man who sells? Wasn't I being specific, not exclusionary? And quite frankly, stopping at every instance to substitute the word 'person' for man or woman is to me, exhausting and unnecessary. And if it's suggesting substitutions for the word "chaste," because, in its digital logic *even a knowledgeable audience might be unfamiliar with this word*, what, big G, might you be suggesting about how knowledgeable a modern audience might **not** be? Certainly, Grammarly is a program I can choose to ignore, but its concerns are just part of a bigger insidious seed change that I feel has taken the culture's good sense these past few years, and it surely involves language.

Not just Grammarly is overreaching, they are only the tip of a quickly melting iceberg. I refer you to Dr. Jordan Peterson's fight against Canada's proposed Bill C-16 legislation, compelling speech, for a truly appalling, heavy-handed attempt at what is, for all intents and purposes, a dangerous trend in the all-inclusive middling, 'deballing' if you might allow me, of what we say and how we say it. And while I don't like to show my hand at what chapters I think are more important in this book than others, I do humbly think that what I am on about here could be pretty damn important to us all, not just sex writers.

I saw this problem writ large in a series of articles I recently wrote about orgasm denial and chastity (there's that "chaste" word again) for what tends to be a feminine-skewed website. I know I could already be welcoming some criticism just for writing the word "feminine," or skewed even…hell, I really don't know anymore! But I don't feel that these words are offensive. In fact, I don't feel any word is offensive, it is the feelings and connotations we attach to certain words that gets everybody's undies in a twist, a point for another time or chapter, certainly.

But "feminine" describes what, in my opinion, is the tenor of the stuff on the site. And please don't get on me for what I mean, don't mean or want to mean by the word "feminine." If you went to the URL of this site I am talking about and had a look-see, surely you might feel differently, which would be super-duper cool with me. As I say we are all entitled to our opinions, just so we are clear here. (Man, this covering your ass stuff at every turn really gets exhausting, doesn't it!?)

Anyway, while I have lots of respect for the site's editor and my fellow writers, and I love reading the stuff that gets posted across the site's many pages, presently my pieces, and plenty of others, are incurring an increasing number of editor's warnings. A simple couple-paragraph 'Language note' of caution is added above so many articles now. The latest warning topping my chastity piece stated that my article *"employed language that was 'intentionally gender non-specific,' and that words like words 'cock' and 'penis' are used with absolutely no gender specificity assigned to any term."*

I don't even know what that all means or why anybody would have to be warned about it.

I'm one of those heart-on-my-sleeves guys, very sensitive to other people's feelings. I cry at commercials and the first notes of a song can bring me to my knees in an uncontrollable memory recall. The very last thing I'd ever want is a reader feeling uncomfortable from my use of some word or to misconstrue my meaning when I know I would never intentionally seek out to exclude/hurt/bother anybody.

Really, my stuff doesn't need a warning.

Yes, I publish a lot of erotic satire, and it can be biting at times. But I never attack those who cannot defend themselves, and I am never mean for mean's sake, a tenet of writing I learned from old Jonathan Swift, one of the greatest satirists of all time. Really, most times, especially in my non-fiction writing, I am hoping to make my reader — be they a person with a penis or not — feel a bit freer about their sexuality and maybe consider something that they might not have yet tried.

Or, at least, consider not judging somebody who is trying something that the reader might find personally repellent.

It's all about spreading the love around my side of the street, and again, I'm really not the writer you need be warned about. And damned or canceled though I might be for saying it, I don't think anybody should be warning any reader about any writer (except a warning on adult material to warn away children under the age of 18). And again, I feel, no word is, in and of itself, offensive.

I guess what I am saying here is that I am pretty damn "triggered" over the fact that the public at large might get triggered by something I write or say. Come on, are we so weak that now in writer's guidelines I have to read that editors want writers to set warnings in cover letters about possible stuff in a submitted piece that might make them verklempt? (Yes, I have seen too many writers guidelines like this in the past year).

First of all, how the hell do I know what's going to set you off? Secondly, if I am submitting a horror short story to a fiction magazine asking for horror stories, the editor should just assume he or she (no, I won't use 'they' when referring to a single person…get over it!) might be reading some horrible stuff. If you want me to warn you that there is sex in the story, yeah, I'll give you that. This happens plenty to me as I like to mix genres as you know, and in the case of erotica and horror they are oft-familiar bed fellows. And lots of genre mags like their genre unmuddied, wanting robots, spaceships, etc. but no nookie in a sci-fi tale or devils and spirits in a horror tale, but not sexy devils or spirits. But beyond this, you might just be in the wrong business if you are so easily triggered by the very gristle of what you are asking for.

To my way of thinking, being "triggered," annoyed, or pricked, is good. Art can entertain as well as challenge, and I'd say, yes, let us stumble upon that which makes us think or presents a completely 180-degree view from our own. Let us get pissed off, write letters (or tweets and twats) about that which gets our blood boiling. Who needs stories, poetry and non-fiction opinion pieces that agree with us all the time?

It's too boring to be given that which does not needle our sensibilities from time to time.

But it's a wacky world we live in presently folks. The powers-that-be running websites, publishing magazines, even teaching in our schools worry so much about offending **anyone** that they bend over backward, making sure to include **everyone**. They over-explain, consistently apologize, and over-compensate for offenses they assume are being leveled at every turn. And of course, as I do for most everything these days, I blame social media for making us all so hypersensitive. Strike that....so bloody *weak*!

We presently live locked deep in Pauly Shore a la carte Opinion-Domes made to our making. We don't let in anything we haven't well-vetted or might slip to the side of what we only think we want. And the minute we read/see or hear something that offends us we not only have the opportunity to get online to express our feelings to the world (and somehow assume the world gives a toss) but all too soon somebody or somebodies are going to tweet us back in agreement. Then we have a cause, a backing of the like-minded, a fuel to our righteous indignation and watch out world, we be a'comin!

The way this used to work was a buddy or our partner would come into the bar, café or bedroom huffing and puffing about something, have his or her say about what got them all so worked up, maybe a few of your group would agree, or you'd reach out to give your lover a hug, then a beer would be passed, maybe a little quick nookie would commence and the moment/offense/rude word your person was all churned up about would be forgotten. It didn't linger. It didn't get Tickity-Tocked. It didn't become a thing, something to "cancel," or to have a cultural movement about. Whatever it was that got us going we accepted as either one person's opinion, a divergent political view, somebody's tirade or an artist's expression. But it never really worked its way in all that deeply because we were tougher, we were more prone to let crapola (and let's face it, all of this really is crapola, don't take the world so seriously kids!) roll off our backs. We didn't instantly hear the echo of so many others with nothing better to do now with their time than be offended coming back at us.

Contrary to the walking-on-eggshells approach so many of us presently adopt when reacting with our fellow humans, I tend to have lots of faith in the intelligence and reason of my brothers and sisters. And I am especially assured of the everyday reader's sensibilities. I believe that even when somebody encounters something that rankles them or lands completely counter to their belief system, most have the mature ability to digest, consider, and then move on.

That's if we stay off social media or don't get wrapped up into thinking we are the center of the universe, even for a split second.

Doesn't this all come down to the old 'sticks and stones' axiom? Isn't there more important things happening in your world than to get all twisted by a word or even an idea that you don't like or agree with? And really, if you are prone to such deep feelings of revulsion over what you read or see, dare I say, a pre-article warning, Disney's seeming ubiquitous warnings on classic cartoons isn't going to diffuse you much.

I wrote a story recently, where a lady (yes, an actual biological born female…wait, hold on, is it ok for me to write 'biological female?' must I use some other new term over acronym or run the risk of getting castigated?) was looking for a right good humping to the exclusion of anything else. It was thought by the editor who sent the story back to me that my lady was exhibiting harmful stereotypical behavior, that I had not written her with enough complexities. Not that I would ever do so with a rejection, but I could have easily argued that some ladies, as some men, as some transgender people, as some, well….lots of humans, just love to, ya know, to do it!

And for some of us, and certainly, for the sake of my story (an erotic story at that), it was all about this person 'gettin' some' across the course of my pages.

Some characters have lots more layers to them, but some do not. Believe me, with my writing you are going to have to be happy or move on. I'm not that great of a writer where I can create such rich characters in a short story that rival those concocted by a Poe, a Hemingway, or even an E.L. James. And I assure you, in writing a lady mainly motivated to seek a good Rodgering I wasn't making a blanket statement about heterosexual females, as this editor came right out and told me he felt I was.

And please, don't argue that I was attempting an unconscious strike against heterosexual women (or should I use the word "Cis" here?). That's just silly talk. And even if this *was* my point, that I believe all hetero females mainly want to have sex to the exclusion of all else, so... the...f...what!?

Grow up. (Yeah, I guess I do sound a little angry, huh?) I can express and live to my dying day with this opinion — an opinion I state again, that I do not have — and you can choose to hate me for it, if that was my opinion. But can't we still be buds, go for coffee, even have a little bouncy-bouncy on occasion? As grown-ups, I think we know, or at least should realize, that we don't have to agree with or like the opinions of others, to still hang with, get along with, even have sex with someone with different views than us.

Or are we too far gone into our tribes these days that we can't allow for this schism?

It's ok. I took the rejection and moved on. But I didn't change my character and how she acted nor my suspicion that the current climate isn't allowing for so many gray areas these days and people are too often rushing to snap judgments.

Look, I'm not a complete doody head, and my apologies for appropriating doody headism. I fully understand that there are great big groups of folks who have felt marginalized for a very long time. Many people have not had a voice in our global culture until recently where many minorities now seem to have gained some push-back and power across cultural lines. This is fantastic. I want everyone to be happy, to feel that they matter, to pursue their goals, just as long as their pursuit doesn't encroach on anybody else's pursuit. But looking for something to be there that's not, from a lousy old writer like me, is lots of wasted time. Being ready to jump at any provocation, or what's worse, getting your panties in a twist — and I'm sorry, if I am excluding those of us who do not wear panties — over an offense you simply could never really feel given your experience, gender, or ethnicity, falls well into the category of virtue signaling to me.

And while we are on the subject of marginalized populations, let me offer another too-far pendulum swinging I have been noticing in the multitudinous small press, anthology fiction calls, and one-act play guidelines I have been getting.

Never before have I noticed the glut of publications calling for fiction strictly from what the people behind-the-scenes consider "minority" writers — the acronyms alone that are used here make my head spin — while excluding other writers. Again, I get it. The editors here feel they are playing catch-up, righting a wrong, reaching out to give certain people a chance who have never had that chance. But I fear that this kind of inclusion creates more of a separation between people and the propagation of a myopic view, just as dangerous when minorities weren't invited to play in the sandbox of life.

And believe me, I am even fearful that a diatribe like this chapter, any questioning or criticism against current societal norms will get one (me in this case) labeled as being against the good fight, freedom, all people's rights. Which I am not.

How about the rain/reign of guano that might come down on us when we write a story where partners engage in and enjoy degradation, something your characters consent to when playing their kink games? Given the powder keg culture we currently straddle our firm buns upon, it's not such a stretch I feel for a writer to come under fire for writing fiction where one person in a sexual relationship calls another a "Slut," or raises a racial epithet during bed play because their partner agrees that this kind of emotive language is perfectly fine to use, and indeed turns them on. Extrapolating from this, when will the censoring end? What if the language you use is considered, by current standards — and God knows these goalposts move all the time — offensive?

Or let's take what just happened, as I write this, to classics of literature, a sure scourge perpetrated, I am sad to report, by the authors' own publishers and estates.

It was announced that both Roald Dahl and Ian Fleming were seeing an 'update' of their language in new printings of their books. Hoping for more inclusion/diversity/equality from these authors, the companies that own the Dahl and Fleming oeuvres employed "sensitivity readers" (and if that term doesn't get my goblets a'churning in full Orwellian overdrive, nothing will!) to excise words like "fat" and "ugly" (from Dahl) and portray James Bond's interaction with people of an ethnicity not his with a modern-day sensitivity. Effectively bastardizing classics of popular literature, to my way of thinking this is simply censorship in the guise of the modern malady of presentism. Can't modern readers digest words like "fat," "ugly," and "mad," used in the original *Charlie and the Chocolate Factory* to describe the nasty kids Wonka has to endure? Do the readers of James Bond's classic exploits have to be warned that the possible circumstances, descriptions and depictions in these tales, written years ago and portraying events set in times just as far in the past, might prick their more evolved (again, substitute 'weak') sensibilities?

Wah, wah, wah, I say.

It's not just altering an author's intended language by people who have no business doing so, or Disney throwing up a pre-cartoon warning every now and again. No, what worries me most is that the populace is so weak-kneed, so easily offended, all too ready to be led, and poised to strike fueled by an epidemic-wide conceit that all language and thought are suspect and therefore worthy of cutting down willy-nilly.

Am I splitting hairs? Oh Chim-Chim, I only wish I was!

Being a writer about it, I have encountered the debate over the use of the word *cum* over *come* (both are perfectly acceptable to me, without any judgment made); if writing out words like "smat," "swish," and "slurp" betters our fiction or slows it down; if one should be capitalizing the words Mistress or Master; should I be changing my spelling of folks to folkx or as I mentioned a few paragraphs ago, and something I won't do, including 'they' more than 'he' or 'she?' These considerations, while part and parcel of life these days, are minor to my mind, when my real concerns about the language, as you see above, run deeper.

In a very real way, I think Martin Niemöller's famous "First they came for…" poem could be well applied to any worker of words, as much to anybody expressing their opinion/art/thought these days. Surely, Niemöller was writing about a scourge on humanity the likes of which this planet has never seen again…thank a good God I don't readily believe in. But watch out for the words you use, or the thoughts you have and how you express them, and what might become of you for that expression.

Go forth and be happy, my little droogs. That's all I could ever want for you and yours. And don't take life so seriously. Words cannot, in and of themselves, offend, and remember well that quip about opinions and our buttholes…we all have them, and the potential stinkiness for both is great.

Sorry, did that offend you?

19.

The Consideration Of Adopting A Nom De Plume And What Not Doing So Might Cost You

We writers of naughty words often get a bad rap. First of all, we scribble sex stories. Secondly, it's often assumed we, you-know-what while scribbling those stories. Thirdly, we are often criticized for exercising the stuff we write about on our unsuspecting dates and partners. And lastly — and this is surely the prevailing wisdom I hear uttered all the time — since we write naughty words, we can't write anything else. None of the above is true in my case, as I'm sure it's not true in many a writer's case, but professionally, as well as personally, writers of erotica face stigma.

And because of this stigma the big question dirty word writers all too often have to consider (beyond where do I sell these naughty stories) is should I engage a nom de plume?

As with everything else, there are arguments to be made pro and con on this score. Lots of writers choose pseudonyms when they genre hop. Anne Rice is famous for writing her spank free-for-all "Beauty" series as A. N. Roquelaure, her mainstream erotica as Anne Rambling, and her supernatural stuff as Anne Rice, although she outed herself years ago over this identity conundrum in her brilliant book *Belinda,* a story about a children's book writer/illustrator coming to terms with his work taking on a more erotic bent.

I've never used anything but my real name on every piece of writing I create, having penned reviews for Pyrex dildos, managed a couple pieces for Cesar Milan, and in my children's books, to name some of the stuff I'm into. Then again, I'm not in the league where I've yet encountered even a smidgen of Anne Rice-ian popularity (nor will I ever), but I am sure the landscape changes when things get to that level.

I once met a woman in one of my writing classes who told me she penned sexy Christian fiction. Who knew there was such a thing? Then again, where else do other Christians come from if at least some of them aren't having sex? Although one might assume one might want to cloak one's identity Romulan-like when penning this kind of stuff, this lady said that since the niche was recognized and enjoyed, albeit by a small section of the faithful population she ran with, she let it be known who she was and how she could be found.

Among all the kinds of writing I do, I am half of a duo, with my illustrator friend/partner of a self-published series of children's books. In trying to spread awareness of these books, my partner and I present live sing-a-long/draw-a-long/read-a-long programs based on the 16 titles we have produced over the past four years. And like the aforementioned naughty Christian fiction lady writer, I use my real name on everything I write, adding the "Jr." to my writing, keeping it off my music making. But having my real name out there my partner and I ran into trouble when a teacher went to research us beyond our electronic press kit (and why she did this I have no idea) stumbling as she did upon my name and all the dirty stuff I've written. This disturbed said lady enough to halt all further communication with us. We wouldn't be playing in her particular reindeer games, which translated to mean, she wouldn't be hiring us to come to her school.

This is surely the bane of all smut scribbles who also write 'mainstream' stuff. And it doesn't just have to be people fretting about the great chasm between children's literature and porn. This trepidation over being 'outed' has happened to me plenty before, like when a mining machine part maker or a naturopath learned about my 'other' bona fides and questioned the logic of working with me, although they both came aboard after I showed them plenty examples where I wrote non-naughty stuff for web pages, brochures, articles, and books. Still, I have never, nor will I ever, write under a nom de plume, or anonymously, other than when I'm hired to ghostwrite a book, webpages where I am not expecting a byline, and maybe if I ever get around to a memoir.

I am not so obtuse not to understand what got into the teacher's jumper to leave her skittish, but when reasoned further, I don't see why folks like her, and so many others, can't come to the following logical conclusions about us writers writing smut as well as anything else:

1.) Like most adults, I entertain adult thoughts, and yes, some are sexual, and in my case, I come to write about them from time to time.

2.) As any reasoned adult would, I know that adult fare, thoughts, pictures, texts and ideas, certainly those of a sexual nature, are not to be shared with children. As I write this, we are having hefty debates in the U.S. over the nature of what should and should not be taught in elementary schools, especially in regard to sex/gender matters. And although I am rather free-thinking in most areas of social concerns, I do bristle at what exactly we might be teaching our kids, and at what age. I champion that, where sex is concerned, even in an educational context, we should well consider what we expose our kids to, and at what age.

3.) If you were to take even the most cursory look at the children's books that my partner and I produce, you won't find even a hair of suggestiveness. This is deliberate. When we set out to create our series, we pledged to stay away from the double entendre, the 'wink-wink-nudge-nudge' of cartoons that play as much to kids as they do adults, to avoid innuendo. You could never confuse what we do with anything that even tickles the salacious in any way. Call us silly, sure, maybe even slightly didactic with themes about friendship, being true to yourself, and realizing the wonders of the world around you. But there is no hint of sexuality in any of our stuff.

4.) I am trying to make a living here, and while maybe not a traditional job, this writing thing I do is my profession, and I take it somewhat seriously. Therefore, it is in my best interest since I have the talent to do so, or have bamboozled enough people into thinking I do, to work my work in any which way I can work.

5.) I don't think I have to adjust the way I do things for your comfort. As much for reasons 1–4 as the fact that *you* having a problem with the way in which I work is *your* problem. I don't feel there is any reason to hide, and frankly, I pretty much don't want to. I'm not being smug here, I just want the freedom accorded to me that I accord to everybody else.

So, I write porn and children's books. Ok, and your point is?

I also play acoustic-based-instrumental as well as heavy rock music. I have published poetry, articles, and press releases. I am even the co-host of a podcast…although, who doesn't have a podcast these days? I have as much written and seen produced my family-friendly historically-based one act plays as I have penned, performed and emceed an adults-only cabaret of song and sketches. I write plenty of cross-genre fiction where I mix many styles, themes, and action in one story and have ghostwritten books for heads of corporations, dentists, and ex-porn stars.

I worked as a freelancer for one of the biggest porn news companies in the world, as much as I have written web copy for a sourdough bread maker. I'm a hack, as I say here over and over, in the very best sense of that word. I go where the work is. Do I do all of this writing equally well? Probably not. Do I like writing a wide variety of stuff? Damn skippy! Do I care a wit about your opinion of me? Well, I'd rather we get along, and I'd like to think if you bought something from me, that you'd be happy with the read or listen. But in the end, no, I don't care so much for the opinion of people who don't know me or don't come to like my work for a reason other than the work. Sorry, but this is true.

All you need to know is that if you hire me for a job, I will deliver what you have hired me for to the best of my ability as I will always endeavor to give my best to any writing, or song, I put my metaphorical pen to.

So, what's in a name, really? Not much as far as I am concerned. The work, each piece of it, should speak for and by itself, naughty or not.

20.
How Do You Create A Character?

Alice Walker, author of *The Color Purple* among other wonderful works, claimed that her characters revealed themselves to her as she wrote. The equally wonderful writer Ursula K. Le Guin pretty much said the same about her fictional people, they came and told her their story, revealed their names, simply reported to her their lives as she wrote. The spectacular modern noir fiction writer James Sallis claims he simply listens to a character when they reveal themselves to him as he writes.

Haven't I been saying all along, that to write, you have to, well, um… get to writing?!

In the many ways I feel erotica is different from other forms of writing, it's not so different on the how/why and what of character creation. We naughty scribblers often create folks we really wish we could meet, or we have our characters act out scenarios we fantasize or we invest them with qualities we wish our lover might suddenly show.

Other times, we set the people who populate our fictions to work out that which we have already experienced, but have yet to come to terms with. Given the nature of what erotica can be, the more extremes of particular human frailties and graces often play loud and proud across our characters actions and speech, then again, some of the very best erotica I have ever read, even written, has featured characters who display their motivations and emotions in very subtle ways.

However you create your peeps, from mixing-and-matching real character studies into fictional ones, using Willy Wonka's favorite "pure imagination" or dumping out a bunch of scribbles you have written across a Starbucks napkin of some folks you observed in the wild, the process of creating characters could be the same for you each time you sit down to write or take on a wholly different form for each of your stories. You might as much suddenly find somebody forming across your page via dialogue as they could be born from a setting you create. The people of your fictions, plays, narrators of your lyrics, wise old sages of your prose poems might burst upon you when you least expect, or they can be folks you have seen in your mind's eye for a very long while.

The point is, they come from everywhere in so many ways.

As I reread this short chapter, I feel I owe you an apology for not really being able to give you much about the nuts and bolts of character creation. What I *can* offer is that when your people pop up or you finally manage to get right that fantasy you had for your tenth-grade librarian releasing her top bun, you have to be ready to pull up a chair, let your guys, girls, space aliens and whatever-have-you sit right down and tell you their story. They want 'in' on what you are creating and it's your job to give them life.

From a Hannibal Lecter to a Huck Finn to *Little Women*'s Jo March, characters drive story either because they reflect our hopes and dreams or live lives very much like ours. And while I can't rightly tell you how to create yours, I can say you really can't have worthwhile readable fiction without good characters. The people who come to populate my scribbles are as much amalgamations of the wide range of folks near and dear to me as they create themselves whole cloth from my brain. If they have been hiding out in my imagination for some time, or if the action of my story births them, I have no idea. But without my characters, I know there wouldn't be much reason to read me.

And even then, I still fear there's not much reason to read me.

21.
Be Nice

I had finally finished writing a book that was very near and dear to my heart. A non-fiction exploration of what I felt were thirteen overlooked 1970's prog-rock albums. This tome was as much a labor of love as it was, I knew, far from what I usually write and have come to sell. But progressive 1970 music pumps deep in my heart, the writer and musician I am has been informed so much from these sounds, and I have even managed a fair amount of music writing (you can check www.vintagerock.com, if you are so inclined).

My long-story-short explanation here is that this new book meant a lot to me.

I also knew it covered a niche subject, and to find a publisher I'd have to come across a press specializing in not just music, but music of specific rock genres. And while yes, there are some out there, they are few and far between.

Hell, you think erotica is a hard sell? Getting this book bought was going to be even tougher! It would also help, I knew, to exploit (in the best way possible) any relationships I may have made through my reviewing/musical connections. And I did just that, contacting an author I quite admire, who pounds out music books (and long detailed ones at that) at a ridiculously prodigious rate. He usually tackles one subject at a time — a famous band's history, an unusual off-shoot genre of rock — and because I have interviewed him for Vintage Rock and have had occasion to buy some of his books, we have emailed a bit in the past.

So, I figured, let me ask this guy's advice about my new book.

Did he know of a good publishing house I could drop my 30 thousand + words with? Could he offer anything really that might help pivot me, even slightly, in the right direction?

He categorically refused to help.

His email was cordial enough, but he actually said, "I don't do that," when I asked him to recommend a publisher. He also added in a slightly succinct, but surely off-putting manner that my book was dead-in-the-water, given the subject, when I barely even hinted to him what the book was about.

'Ok, so that's just one guy Ralph,' I hear you say 'What do you care?'

Well, I do care.

When that big-time music author emailed me back in that way *and I still don't get his, "I don't do that." Did he mean he won't recommend other music book writers to possible publishers because he doesn't want the competition? This dude is light-years ahead of anything I could ever possibly catch up to!* it took me aback. Ok, we aren't friends, he doesn't owe me old Rickard Olla (as in nothing much at all, Richard 'dick olla,' get it?) but a little advice or encouragement would have been nice.

Nice.

Nice.

I've said it before, and I will say it again: BE NICE.

To whomever emails you, calls, says "hi" at a book signing, be you lucky enough to have one and it's attended by anybody other than your family and friends. Be cordial and give a moment of your time to someone who might want to gab a bit after a writing class you've just given at a kink convention. I am here to tell you, being nice will play long and sweetly through your life and rep. while being mean, or just stand-offish, won't.

And being nice makes you feel so freaking good. Come on, why be a dick?

I once had a very *nice* lady meet me outside the hotel where a weekend kink convention was being held and that I was as much attending as teaching at with my buddy, M. Christian. As I told you, we've been invited to a few of these gatherings to give forth our knowledge of this or that subject and this young woman approached me over the writing class Chris and I had given that very morning.

Being the friendly, approachable *nice* guy I always am, of course I took the time to talk to this bright-eyed woman who had gone out of her way to seek me out, just to tell me how much she had enjoyed our class. She leveled me (and I mean leveled me where I was nearly rocked back on my heels) telling me how what I had said in class had given her a new way of looking at her own writing. She asked for a hug, which I, of course, welcomed, thinking 'Well, how much better could things get than this?!' I had made a difference in somebody's life, in their writing with some dumb words I had managed to utter during a hour-and-a-half casual hang this convention called a class. Yes, I have told you how wonderful these classes always were and how much Chris and I got out of them. This woman complimenting me so wonderfully, and her sure warm hug, was clear testament to a job well done.

Do you remember the movie *Roadhouse*? Yes, the one where dearly departed Patrick Swayze plays "Dalton," a bouncer in a rough and randy club where Jeff Healey (another dearly departed soul) plays nightly behind chicken wire. In that movie, Swayze says to the bouncers, that no matter what happens with the rowdy customers, always BE NICE. Take "Dalton's" advice here, be nice. *Also check out the movie for its unbelievable homoerotic undertones, they are startling in their frequency in such a mainstream popcorn flick.*

This is more than just a 'don't burn a bridge' lesson. And I hate to admit this though I must, and I hope what you may have realized by now…I am a nice guy. In fact, I pride myself on being so.

That lady approaching me at the kink convention needn't have ever worried that I wouldn't be anything but tickled pink by her approbation, and her wanting a few minutes with me. And I'll admit something even deeper. As I get older those kinds of moments matter to me more and more. Call it me sniffing the certain carrion stink of my mortality wafting across my personal imagined river Styx or that I just get softer around the edges the more testosterone I lose, but the one-on-one with people, making connections, transitory though they might be and being appreciated for what I do as much as letting people I appreciate them in kind is growing ever more important to me.

What I am on about here in this sickly sweet rainbows and unicorns diatribe is a suggestion on how you should deport yourself as an author, regardless of your age, popularity, gender or ethnicity. This BE NICE stuff is really meant for your everyday gettin' around, be it with a work colleague, a fan, or your sibling.

Just BE NICE.

In the end what's it gonna cost you? And the difference your niceness can make in somebody's life might just get you that hug.

22.

5 Red Flags To Look For When Searching For Writing Jobs

Part of the freelance writing life, at least mine, unagented as I am, and writing across lots of formats and genres (it's not all just chocolate sauce dripping on robots' nipples with me) is to be consistently looking for writing jobs, as I have mentioned plenty here. And while you might indeed find many a good one in your searching, don't be fooled, there are lots of writing jobs being advertised right now that are right shite.

In fact, plenty are designed to rip off a writer.

How then does one cut the fat from the meat, keep from falling into the trap of spending time, energy, and sometimes even money on an employer that is not going to pan out?

Here are five red flags to be on the lookout for in potential writing jobs.

1. **You see the same ad over and over.** Craig's List seems to be the lowest common denominator for most things and one could argue that if you see someone calling out for a writer on Craig's List, this should be a red flag in and of itself. I think I land one job out of the twenty there that I send resumes to, still, it is a place I do check on occasion. But if the same ad for freelance writing is posted from the same employer a few times a week (or every day as I see some ads) there might a real good reason, and a red flag, why this position isn't ever filled. I tend to think it's less that the employer has a ton of work, as more likely that they are either seeing a consistent turn-over of writers (ask yourself why), or they aren't really looking to hire anybody as they are hoping you'll click further into their supposed employment questionnaire so they can grab you as a subscriber or hit you with some other advertisement. RED FLAG.

2. **They ask for specific samples.** This is not an absolute RED FLAG, but I have come across lots of would-be employers asking for samples.

What always prompts my suspicion here is that it would be all too easy to cull a bunch of these samples from writers hungry for work, which most writers are, amass a bunch of free pieces then never have to pay anybody.

3. The payment is unspecified or "contingent upon." Sorry, but there are tons more net businesses and those 'going-to-be-the-next-big-thing' ideas then there are those that become genuinely successful. Waiting for your pay contingent upon how much or how well a new site sells views, downloads, etc. or not ever given a set price for work, or a would-be employer seemingly reluctant to negotiate one, are sure RED FLAGS. The employer here might not be dishonest, per se, but simply not competent or simply underfunded, or just, well…stupid.

4. They take forever getting back to you. In this day and age, as I mention all the time, there is no reason not to get back to someone in a timely manner. If, of course, getting back to somebody in a timely manner matters. If good communication does not matter to your possible employer, RED FLAG, then it shouldn't matter so much that you work for them.

5. Their secondary departments are not working well…or at all. Furthering from the above — I once began to work for a very large, well-known publication and when I tried to contact their accounting department on a mini matter, welcomed to do so as I was from an email someone from their accounts payable department sent when I began working for them, I never heard back from the publication's payment office. I sent three emails…and called, again as I was welcomed to do so in that initial email and this was a huge company. RED FLAG, if an employer's departments are unresponsive or not speaking to each other.

6. (Yeah, I know I said five but I actually wrote six. Sue me!) **Even if they do get back to you in a timely matter, neither of you know what the hell the other is talking about!** This is no small point and something I have encountered more than once. From my experience, there is usually nothing malicious here, the employer isn't trying to be obtuse, it's just that we come to a communication loggerhead. Even if two people want to work together and a good amount of the preliminary is figured out, there are simply those times that even the most reasoned and well-intentioned employer and

employee can't seem to understand what the other wants.

I have been in this pickle a few times where my writing just doesn't hit the mark the employer was hoping for, even after I have been paid, or I just can't seem to figure a vision forward for what's needed, despite how much the employer and I come to talk about it. This is not a true RED FLAG situation but if you should see the flags of constant misunderstandings starting to unfurl, you and the employer should know enough to part company before things really get difficult for you both.

Yes, I know you want to work. I know the writing jobs are few and far between. I know you are doing your best to stay open, honest and NICE. But not all jobs are for all people or are even worth pursuing. And some jobs are, at their core, out to rip you off. Watch for the flags.

23.

O Brave New World With Such Things In It: When I Talk To My Laptop, It Types What I Say!

It's not the first time, nor will it be the last, that I have come to some technological breakthrough so late that it is no longer regarded as a breakthrough.

I'd been contemplating computer dictation programs for some time. Knowing plenty of people who use them, I wondered if this way of 'writing' could be helpful to me. But, as with most everything I try to bring myself up to speed on, I feared learning to use my Windows' dictation program would be a long hard slog. As with most things in my life, I suspected I'd grow so frustrated that in the end, I'd just chuck the idea halfway through. It's not that my time is so precious — it really isn't — it's just that I don't have the brain capacity, even a tiny amount of it, for anything technical. You should see me trying to figure out a train schedule through a phone app! Give me human emotions or routing round the possibilities of my fellows' future next moves, and I can offer better intel than most. But have me turn on my computer to navigate even two pages of a job application, and I'm a goner.

So, you can bet I had trepidation over this voice-activated thingie.

I needn't have been so worried. Sure, I couldn't get the damn program to work in Word, but after a quick video tutorial from a rather sweet and smiley UK author lady, I was on my way to voice activation via Google Docs. And although GD is not something I use all that often, I am slightly familiar with the program from some work I did for a client who wanted me to work in Google Docs exclusively (and in coming to edit this very book). So, now, I can say something, and the computer types it for me.

But…

Will I use this new tool? Will dictating be better/faster/easier for me than writing? In the tutorial, the smiley blonde also showed how one could dictate into one's phone via GD. Will I take advantage of this option when I am out and about? As she said, she knows she looks slightly bonkers to people around her when talking into her phone for long periods. But what does she care? She's a writer, this is what we do. We get an idea and by hook or by crook we have to get it down. God knows I open up the Gmail app on my phone all the time, typing quick letters to myself that contain only a turn of phrase or a title I want to remember, and then send it to myself. As far as me talking to myself when I'm out and about? Hell, I do this all the time anyway, as I've mentioned and I'm not dictating anything, just talking out loud to keep myself company.

My current journey into computer program unknowns started this very fine morning with an idea prompted by a few back-and-forth emails I was led into the night before. I won't 'out' the recipient of those emails, but his less-than-interested replies prompted quite the chunky thought in my mind that begot another and then…well, you know how this can get with us writers.

A noodle of an idea will all too quickly ignite a whole idea or long fictional scene, and then you just have to go get a pad and pen or plop yourself in front of your laptop. I reasoned that the idea starting to formulate in my pasta-addled brain might be the perfect opportunity to dictate instead of typing. Why I thought this, I have no idea, but I woke up in the morning today and thought I'd try to make this all a reality.

Now I am not so sure it's a good idea.

Terror of technical conundrums aside, I have had plenty of good steam ahead ideas dissipate behind me like an old locomotive's flaccid plume more often than I can count, and this might be yet another one of them. My first attempt to 'write' this way, sitting back, closing my eyes, and speaking out loud as I managed just before starting this chapter, came forth in what I could only describe as a "confessional" puke. It felt like I was journaling, sitting across from a therapist, actually, and this kind of me-centric pontificating is about the worst sort of word-smithing I can think of.

Using a sure healthy amount of satire, setting stories in faraway places or employing lots of fantasy scenes, I hide in/through my words like most writers do. The first-person pontificating, made all too popular by the personal blogging epidemic, is not the kind of writing I find entertaining. And it's certainly not the kind of writing I want to produce. Sure, it is addicting to give forth in this way, but Anne Frank's diary aside, I feel most of the personal ruminations that come out of our heads and through our fingers are better left unread, especially those of a deep confessional form.

Have you heard the joke about Anne Frank's diary? I am paraphrasing here, but the gist is, 'Hey, if Anne Frank's diary is so great, why was there never a sequel?' I know, I know, it's tasteless, still, it makes me laugh every time I think of it. Share it as you dare.

Sure, write it, get it out all you want, but your (or my) feelings on a matter aren't going to be all that interesting unless we can spin them into some sort of entertaining three-minute country song or some wild sci-fi sex romp with layers of meaning. I will concede that there are writers who can give forth their feelings in their writing and surely produce gold, but the Joan Didions and even the Anne Franks of this world are few and far between.

I guess my point here (beyond how much of a scourge to the art form of writing personal blogging has become) is that not all new ideas will work for us, as much as some may. So, I'll give voice activation another go; see if I can produce more than just a lengthy screed on my ick-producing feelings. But I'm leery and not prone to positiveness. Didn't Voltaire show us how dangerous it is to go through life like Candide?

I do have to admit though, I can see how the voice activated program might be perfect when I am interviewing someone. I'll be able to just push the speaker button on my phone and grab with them, catching their answers verbatim. Yes, I know there is a way to do this with a phone app, but I'm going to try voice activation the next time I am set to conduct an interview and see how it serves me.

Look, we all know how annoying auto-correct is getting. And I'm not sure if you have heard yet, but there are the new AI (artificial intelligence) programs that are all the rage.. Science-fiction writers have warned us for years that the machines will come to consciousness and take over the world, and as I write this the brand spanking new ChatGPT programs seem to be encroaching in all fields, certainly creative ones where writers were usually used.

All of the above is hard on us writers. We don't generally get out and about all that much in what we do, so we really are only exposed to what's out there if we allow it in. Presently, it seems, we have to be ever so careful in what we let in or die trying to catch up.

Dictating or not, who knows if and how much of this new way of doing things or any other, is my future, I declare as I actually *type* this.

24.

"Take The Chair On The End": A Writer's Relationship With Words

My longest friendship is between my buddy Tom and me. Like me, Tom is a writer, not of erotica, more satirical pieces, and well-considered wry comic routines. For his day job though, Tom works in a corporate environment, not specifically writing, but in his own way, he comes in contact with words quite a bit. In fact, I'd say Tom is working words more than most at his place of business, and coming to deal with language all the time, or more precisely, how the people around him, and lots of these people are his higher ups or those in HR (and pretty brainy folk as he admits), fail to realize the inaccuracies of the language they use.

Tom and I must have this same discussion about twice a week, about how he was given some new directive or asked to fill out a new inner-office test, to even give his specific department considerations to a legal document, and how so often he finds bad grammar, three sentences used when one would have sufficed and mostly, a clear inaccuracy of words used. Sure, both Tom and I graduated with bachelor degrees in English, we are both voracious readers and we write, and I write for a living. But the problems with the language Tom and I encounter on a nearly daily basis are never anything on the level that would only ever bother an English major. Tom tells me all the time about basic language faux pas, omissions, misconstrued meanings that reveal the writer of the memo, or creator of an emailed test, doesn't even have a basic facility of language, or is just too lazy to check what it is they are writing. And I agree, I find it hard to negotiate the world from what people tell me or write because they are not being even a smidgen precise.

Let me give you an example of this from my own life and the instance that gave this chapter its title.

For a time, I was substitute teaching. It was a pretty good job in that 1.) I worked with little kids, as I asked for and was assigned subbing duties for K-5th grade. From my children's book writing and musical performances, the age of kids I am most comfortable being around and teaching (much as I would be teaching when subbing) is K-5, so this fit perfectly for my sensibilities. 2.) I could work on the days I didn't have too much writing as much as not make myself available those weeks I did 3.) The pay was consistent, and not so bad actually, and I never had to worry about a check bouncing.

In order to work in a public school system though, you need to undergo a criminal background check. I had to be fingerprinted and interviewed by one of the many school principals that make up the chain of elementary schools in my town. I passed all of this with flying colors and yes, when needed, I can clean up ok and the smuggling offenses I was brought to court so many years ago were thrown out in a day when it was determined that the kevas and trillium I was trading in was of such a lower grade it couldn't rightly be regulated. But when I visited the local Board of Ed in my town to fill out the last of the paperwork I ran into one of those language inconsistencies. Actually, I ran into two of them within ten minutes of each other, that made me seem as if I was being overtly obtuse or just plain stupid.

 Coming first to stand before a rather nice lady sitting at her desk in a small office on the ground floor of the building, I was given a clipboard with three forms attached to it, a pen, and her instruction to, "Take the chair on the end, and fill these out."

I turned from the lady who had gone back to her paperwork, figuring her instructions would be followed by yours truly, but found I was facing two chairs, set dead center of the wall behind me. Not seeing how one chair could be the 'end' one any more than the other, I turned back to the lady, tried one of three dimpled smiles I always have locked and loaded in my arsenal and asked:

"Which chair would that be?"

She looked up at me with the most withering stare, obviously thinking 'Why are you being such a pain in my arse here, buddy? Just pick a freaking chair, sit down and fill out those papers so I can get you out of my face as quickly as possible.'

"Sit anywhere," she said, and I took the chair on the left for no reason.

But as I scribbled across the papers and tried to avoid the lady's eye, I thought to myself, why be lazy and say the chair at the end when there clearly was no end chair here and furthermore you don't even care what chair I sit in?

Following this bit of fal-de-ral and fiddle-dee-dee, I descended to the basement of the building to fill out some other piece of paperwork. The lady from upstairs had simply told me to venture down for such and such a form, happy to be free of me after the great 'which chair is at the end controversy of 2018.' The building was small, I could find my way, sooner or later I knew I'd come to the right receptionist, so I descended into the lower depths.

"Just go directly across the hall for that," another comely lass, sitting behind a low desk in an office dead center of the hallway told me after I entered her domain and landed my inquiry.

"Thank you, have a nice day," I said, spinning from her.

See, there's that 'nice' again.

The problem was, when I came back into the hall, and looked across it, there was an office to the right and left, pretty much equidistant across the way of the office I had just emerged from, but none directly across the hallway.

See where I am going with this? It's less a comment on corporate or civil language problems as there are too many of these moments where Tom, me, lots of folks I know who are not even writers, run up against words or directions that confuse us simply because they are not stated clearly or the speaker/writer makes assumptions that we don't.

I'll give you yet another example, something I am coming across more and more and surely sets the bee in my particular bonnet a'buzzing almost daily.

As I wrote many times above, as a freelancer I am always entertaining work, and tend to send my resume to lots of places. Occasionally I will get a response from an employer or whoever is working for an employer looking to place a writer in a vacancy. Just the other day I received another one of the many preliminary profile questionnaires sent out to vet a potential employee. I'm used to these, they ask for a respondent's legal name, if you have ever worked for this particular employer seeking you, if you are a veteran, etc. One odd question though was a follow up to what has become the almost ubiquitous *Are you fully vaccinated?* query.

Following I was asked *Will you be requesting medical or religious accommodation.*

Are you as confused as me? Do I need medical or religious accommodation for…what? I stared at my laptop's screen. Were they inquiring about a health condition I have presently that might be jeopardized or hampered by me working for this possible employer? Was this a way for them to sneak in more inquiry related to the vax question asked before it? Did I foresee impinging on my health in the future? I was polite, but had to ask "I really don't know what you mean by this question."

I was also asked if I was willing to relocate for this job. But never being told where the job was, how could I ever judge something like this? *And, just between you and me no, I'm not relocating for any job.*

This always reminds me of J.F.K.'s famous "We choose to go to the Moon" speech, that he gave while addressing Rice University on America's burgeoning space program. If you remember or haven't ever heard it, Kennedy says at one point, "We choose to go to the Moon in this decade and do the other things, not because they are easy, but because they are hard…"

Yeah, um , J.F.K., what are the other things? Want to be more specific here?

I also have played this specific word meaning game just to piss people off. Yes, I am not above being a bit of a jerk sometimes just to be a jerk, but I do like to spin people slightly over the edge with language. My most recent itching-powder linguistic prodding is when I say to a person or group, pontificating on politics, a subject I still believe should not be spoken about in mixed company, just like sex and religion, that ex-U.S. President Trump is the most significant President the U.S. has had since Lincoln. Man, you should see the steam come out of some people's ears! Yes, I know 'The Donald' is a derisive figure, a man people line up vehemently against or for, and as I write this it looks he might very well run for our Presidential post again. But I pick my words here very precisely. **Significant**, to my way of thinking, and according to The Cambridge Dictionary website means: important or noticeable. You bring a positive or negative spin on the word all you like. But I surely meant, important or noticeable in my statement about Donald Trump.

Yes, I do like to flutter the feathers with a word or two when I can.

One could easily blame texting and tweeting on destroying any real facility we used to have with language, and this malady exists for sure. And, I know most people just want to get through the day, score a coffee, slide through work with as little conversation with anyone around them, get home and veg out watching *Ted Lasso*. And unless you are a writer really, a worker with, and of words, you aren't thinking to ask "Which chair is at the end?" or come to consider a couple words in a dead president's speech from decades ago. But as a writer, words damn well matter. What words you use and how you use them is important. As my good friend Bob says all the time, 'words matter.'

Think about Poe's word choice and repetitiveness in his poem "The Bells," when he writes:

To the tintinnabulation that so musically wells
From the bells, bells, bells, bells,
Bells, bells, bells —

Tintinnabulation? Dude? That's a stellar word choice all on its own that should blow you back in your chair! Then he sets a ringing-like repetitiveness by writing all those bells? Yes, this is old Edgar Allan after all, would you expect anything less? But forget an old classic scribbler like Poe. How about way back from the pop world of 1983, on the Stevie Nicks' penned song "Beauty And The Beast" from her solo album *The Wild Heart*? Nicks is savvy enough to use all forms of the word to (as in too, to and two) in one sentence in this killer ballad.

Yes, kids, you get it all here from Edgar Allan Poe to Stevie Nicks.

Tom and I are not trying to be Mr. Smarty Pants throwing big vocabulary words around just because we can. And the last thing we want to do, especially Tom, I know, is spend any more time on dry interoffice reports and or legal documents than we have to. And my Trump example is reserved for those times I am feeling especially prickly; I really have no dog in the political race of my country or any other, so please don't label me. But don't chastise me when I stop and ask for a deeper explanation on what you have just said simply because you're being lazy with language or trying to move your day along a little quicker.

As writers we should be especially aware of what is possible here, for good and bad in our word choices.

Words matter.

25.

Inspired — Or Sickened — By The Stuff In Your Mental Attic

Presently I unearthed some writing I had been wrestling with for years. I found as much good stuff as bad rereading these pages, cringing at some parts, as much as realizing that with a few tweaks I might be able to get some of it to sing anew. And although this work has been a slow slog so far, rereading and reworking this manuscript is coming to inspire me so much that for the first time in a long while, I feel I might be able to finish it.

Often, it's a good idea to put something away that you may have been spinning your mental wheels over. Sure, there is validity in pushing through, muscling the words, just strapping yourself to your desk and not standing up and away from it until you have ejaculated a thousand words; the actual work of writing. But there are equally those opuses (is it opus'i'?) we do well to put away for a while, hide up in the attic of our mind or on your desktop marked UNDONE MASTERPIECES, that we should come back to later during a good cleaning out.

Sometimes we do not have the skill yet to tackle the thing as well as it needs to be tackled. If writing about true events, sometimes we need a significant stretch of time away from when the events occurred or the people we met during them. Other times, we need to take ourselves from the middle of something to see it clearer, and yes, we even must miss it a little. As much as you'll often appreciate a book, painting, your garden even, differently through the many ages you might experience these things, the passing of years — I avoid the word 'maturity' since it makes me throw up a little in mouth every time I say it — will bring a new perspective to a piece of writing you might have stopped writing.

But don't be surprised, when looking back into something you put away, you come to realize that you might not actually need it anymore. This is the other side of the coin in stepping back from something for a while; you might just have hidden this old stuff away for a reason you didn't, at first, realize, and it will never really sing for you. In re-reading, trying to rework, setting yourself to revising a piece you might just come to the conclusion that you're better served chucking the thing entirely. I know this idea is sacrilege to some, I have read the warnings for writers to never just completely throw something away. But believe me, in some instances, purging can unburden you greatly.

Let me enlighten you on this point with another story from my personal "journey." Don't worry, we are near the end of this book, there won't be many more of these Ralphie asides.

In one way or another, I have been wrestling through the songs I compose, the plays I pen and surely lots of my fiction, trying to write about what, for me, was a spectacular handful of years from my growing up. Having a wonderful memory, both a blessing and a curse I feel in equal measure, I am able to recall my mid-teen years, 14-18 specifically, with blinding clarity. Lots of my writing time has been, as well as continues to be, taken up in trying to recreate, comment, and lovingly render these times into my work. I read somewhere that each writer is obsessed with tackling one central theme, dancing it back into their words over and over, even when he or she doesn't realize it. Such is true with me chasing my teen years to write about.

But I come up short, every time, never able to accurately capture this stuff of whispery interplay. It frustrates the hell out of me, and while sometimes I get close in a song or a play monologue, I can't seem to accurately grasp the feeling of what it was like back during those specific years of my past. It might be because this is all too important to me, it might be that, despite what I pride myself on, my memory isn't all that good. But I think it is more that I am not skilled enough to accurately relate the feelings, smells and sights of the times.

C'est la vie.

So, I let it go. Not enough that I don't dip back to try to tell the story of those years still, but watching the Bruce "Springsteen on Broadway" Netflix documentary, I realized, well, here is a born-and-bred New Jersey songwriter, just like me (ok Bruuuuce is slightly more successful in his songwriting than me), tackling his youth and teenage years in lots of his work. So, I let "The Boss" have this one.

Sure, I don't think Springsteen is worrying all that much about my songs competing with his, I doubt he feels me on his creative tail. But for some reason hearing somebody mine the same kind of themes, from the same environs — Springsteen is older so his references from his youth are more from the 1950s and 60s, mine the 1960s and 70s — took the steam off my obsession. And ironically, as you might suspect, easing back on the pedal of the metal of my mind, suddenly made it easier for me to write about those times. Or at least not care so much that I keep missing the mark.

Hell, old Charlie Chaplin complained all the time how he never made the exact movie he wanted to, how his work came up short all the time. And this is freakin' Charlie Chaplin we are talking about here!

I don't have a clear-cut answer of how to deal with your old stuff, the writing you try again and again to tackle, or even if you should or should not, get up, on it again. Nor can I speak to what you might come to view as an unearthed treasure, as opposed to that which you will come to see as an albatross. But I do know that sometimes there is value in walking away from the unfinished, the cast-off, the stuff that has aggravated you into submission, as much coming back to it to start it anew.

26.
The All Too Necessary Ability To Say "Next"

I lost a job today. I feel kind of shitty about it. I have to be honest. As much because I always need the work as the fact that I now, once again, doubt my abilities. There are a whole host of reasons why I failed to make a connection with this client, an adult toy site, and I can rationalize all I like.

My contact, who had been aces with me all along, took lots of the blame herself, claiming miscommunication and her bosses not really laying out what they needed from the get-go, so she, in turn, couldn't relate those exact needs to me. Still, I feel kinda icky and can't help but get down on my skills.

But I know I need to say: "Next."

This might just be the hardest lesson we need come to, and I don't mean only freelance sex writers. The "Next" rule we could probably all hone to a fine edge. I'm not saying don't reflect on why something didn't work, surely learn from your mistakes, be realistic about your skills. But if you are not able to at least whisper a 'next' and flow past the rejections, you might just get too weighed down by them.

Which I feel myself indeed slipping into even now as I write this. But writing, as it usually does for me, is therapeutic and helps me to work this all out.

The good thing about moving forward is, well, you move forward. You set yourself in motion for something coming down the pike you can't predict. I'm not saying it will be better or worse if and when you find some other guy or girl to take the place of the fuck-buddy who no longer wants you, or that you will come to love the game anew when your chess club revokes your yearly membership. I'm just saying that if you can muster a "Next" at those instances when you are rejected, for whatever reason, you will be ready to snatch, grab and maybe even make a more robust pass at whatever is coming.

And something is always coming.

Another powerful aspect of the "Next" and certainly something I am feeling mostly right now, even stronger than I am the rejection, is that I am no longer fence-sitting. During the past two weeks, surfing the logistics of my new working assignment, delivering the work, I had an uneasy feeling that things were not so hunky-dory. You know how you can sense this, right?

Even in the face of my contact telling me she liked my work, the consistent payment, I felt unease as the weeks passed with how long it was taking for the powers-that-be to get back to me when, in the first week, the work was coming fast and furious, and my contact was riding me to get things done. Sure, I no longer have the job, and this rightly sucks, but I am no longer working the worry stone of "Is everything ok, or is it not?" when I sensed all along something wasn't quite right.

It seems I was right on the money all along. That ill feeling I had that I wasn't hitting the mark proved true.

I also made sure to thank my contact, assure her that she and I are all good, which we are, and to tell her that, if things change, if they want to give me another chance, I am here for further consideration. And I am.

I don't hold grudges or look to spank someone later (well, maybe... that's another story). I know you can't unring a bell, and I would say it's a 99% certainty that I will not hear back from the lady about another job or further work from her higher-ups. But I am indeed always open to have the discussion of working for anyone at any time. As I have mentioned time and again here, in my classes, to friends and co-workers, don't burn that bridge!

So, here I am today, feeling a little dejected, but ok. I just think the lesson of saying "Next" was a good one to impart to you my struggling or maybe even entirely happy erotica writer when I myself have to remember to say it.

"Next."

27.
Aged-Out

It's funny, I wanted to end this book with a light and fun chapter, but my cynical old heart couldn't help but add this one in.

You just might find, having the good fortune of steely DNA or coming to apply the exact prescribed medications in the correct manner, that you live long enough to become obsolete. It's pretty much happened to me. Just tickling into 60 as I am as I write this, I surely feel I do not fit into how the world presently spins, see no value in what our culture deems important, and pretty much eschew technology to the point where I am exhibiting the values of a modern-day Neo-Luddite, as you have read.

This is fine. The out-with-the-old-in-with-the-new is supposed to happen from generation to generation. I have become one of those, "Hey, you kids get your bikes off my lawn" curmudgeons, where very little of anything new has much meaning to me, and how I have done things for so very long has been all but deemed archaic. I get it. To everything, there is a season and all that.

The problem here is that I do not have infinite monetary resources. Not that I'd give up writing or music-making, but you best believe I wouldn't pursue my career in any marketable way if I didn't need to make money. So, trying to still do what I do (and believe me, I feel the dwindling of my faculties every day, so I have no idea how long I will be able to keep doing what I do) becomes infinitely harder in a world I truly no longer understand. But it's less the blisteringly fast changes of technology that stupefy me, as frustrating as those changes can be, but more being aged-out in how the culture presently spins.

Best I am able, I deliver the work I can in the best way I know how, keeping my head down. I won't answer an ad for writing I do not do. I mentioned previously not being able to write social media posts, but I could just as easily add in grant writing, or 'pharma' writing as areas I will never be able to just learn as I go along.

More often than not, I refuse to review books, something I am paid to do from time to time, if that book can only be sent to me in PDF form. I already read way too much sitting at my computer. And if I can help it, I avoid communicating via Zoom, Skype and text if someone agrees to get on the phone with me, or in person if they are close to my area and can meet me for a cup of coffee.

Does the above keep me from work? Certainly. But I can't do my job the best way I can if I make too many concessions for the above. The modern ways of interacting, present societal conventions of behavior kill my spirit every time I try to fit in. I know if I attempt to batter my round peg into these square holes of relating, I'll produce less, in quantity and quality, than that I am capable of.

Let me give you yet another example from my writing life (this is the last one, I promise) something that as much illustrates how I do not fit in anymore, and one of my most annoying modern work ethic pet peeves I have, something I have written about already in these pages. I can't understand, nor can I tolerate, how nobody is communicating all that well when, in this day and age especially, we can communicate the best we ever have.

I work for one very well-known website. I love the writing I do for them and am quite fond of the people I do it for, from my immediate contact to the other editors who come to me from time to time, giving me extra work, to the main boss. They are all nice people, honest and forthwith, when I can get them to be so forth...with...it.

Herein lies the problem. As with many other modern businesses, hell with many other people I have found these days, there seems to be an aversion to answering a direct question. Or in not following up over something someone asks me to do, I do it, and then they don't confirm if they got the thing and it was done to their specifications.

What should I just assume? Everything's okay if I don't hear from you?

Here's another example that actually brought me a great client and continued solid financial compensation.

For a while I was ghostwriting for a company. Boo! The work was very interesting as I got to interview/meet/and write for a whole bunch of different people. I penned memoirs, business primers, some harrowing accounts, from very well-known executives to porn stars to entrepreneurs. I found each story fascinating, as I generally think each person is indeed fascinating in their own way when we take the time to get to know somebody (don't get me started!) and I made some good coin. I also increased my interviewing skills as well as my ability to write in someone else's voice. The thing is, the company I was writing for did not stay on top of their clients. They set up the initial work, got me well connected with the subject, but then kind of stepped well into the background as the book progressed. They didn't even ask me for progress reports, which I initially took as a compliment that they'd leave me be to deliver the manuscript, but came to see how much it irked the client, who usually was paying quite the pretty penny to have a book created.

In two cases, I landed work directly and made one solid friendship from the company's lack of communication with their clients. The result of them not checking, ignoring emails and them actually asking me to handle whatever question the client might be having (I would refuse each time with a humorous "Hey, I'm only the writer!") was that the client only ever communicated with me. For them, I became the sole contact person. And they grew ever more frustrated and distrustful of my employer, so much so that when they came to write another book, they called me directly.

The company's loss, from simply not responding to a few emails, was my gain.

Now, as far as my personal business relating goes, I don't think it's unreasonable to ask that if you hire me to do a job and I have a question about that job, why not hit me back as quickly as you can — sure, I know you're busy setting the world on fire — but when you have the ability of being able to communicate from anywhere at any time, but find it more important to watch a TikTok video about a bunch of dogs jumping into a lake or you think spending time on Twitter is going to actually increase your nascent/nescient business… Don't do this stuff instead of answering a writer asking you what SEO keywords you'd like him to use in your web copy, web copy you keep badgering that writer to deliver. Maybe you should prioritize a little.

Yes, I know I am repeating myself about the terrible communication skills of the present population, but dude…come on…as old Southside Johnny says in one of his more popular tunes, "Talk to me!" I don't need you to tickle my taint with a constant 'job well done.' I tickle my taint daily with the new Ronco 'Taint Tickler and Bass Catcher' thank you very much. But, when you come back to me a week later and tell me this or that copy isn't working for you, well a.) don't be surprised that I am surprised b.) don't expect me to drop everything to get on what you should have got on, or at least told me about, a week ago.

But I'm considering the world as it used to be, not as it is. I am confused by a remote job situation where you have me clocking in six set hours a day but don't mind wasting money paying me for working maybe all of two hours of that time. I don't understand working by committee, where one person, the supposed lead on the project or the website's CEO can't make a final decision. I am stymied by the fact that I am stigmatized when I choose not to indicate a pronoun in my byline or a job application. I can't understand why…

Yeah, yeah, yeah, I'm just old, I know. I should just shut up, pull my blanket to my chin. Sorry, to have bothered you. I'm going to leave right after *Matlock* and catch the "early bird special" at the diner.

CONCLUSION

In her 1922 poem "Sacred Emily," Gertrude Stein has some fun with old Willy S.'s "A rose by any other name would smell as sweet" by writing "Rose is a rose is a rose is a rose."

I always interpreted Stein as offering the simplistic view that the thing is just the thing, nothing much more. In my trials and tribulations that you read about above, in pretty much all parts of my life, I try to apply this practical view to the thing I make as I do in making it. Sure, I feel this writing work I do is important, I love doing it, but it's just a thing, as is what it produces. The process is not mystical to me, heaven sent, nor is the end result to be revered.

What we writers make is no more important to the world than a plumber coming to unclog your drain. And just so we are clear here, if your plumber isn't around when you find your toilet overflowing, you surely will feel his absence more than mine if I never write another spanking story.

Furthermore, as you have read throughout this book, I feel we are all artistic. Some of us pursue an art that, if we are successful doing it, we will indeed gain some modicum of the aforementioned audience. Others, like your neighbor who keeps a magnificent garden, is not somebody whose art is seen by a larger population, even though they might have grown the most beautiful garden in a thirty-mile radius. That which you do that fuels your heart, that you define yourself by, that you dream of and attempt to do even when working a full eight-hour day five days a week away from it, is pretty much your art, no more or less important than Picasso painting his weird cube-y nudes.

Again, this doesn't mean that this writing thing I do and maybe you do is not important, it surely is, but no more than anything else; a rose is a rose is a rose and all that.

Lastly — and really I feel this last point has never been more important because of the climate we are presently in — can everybody just take a breath, push away from all digital connecting and amp it down a notch?

Really. What you feel about what you hear, see, taste and smell, might matter to you, but I know for a fact, that the world doesn't give an overall donkey's dingle about how you were offended over a recent tweet or that you simply have to show everyone what you had for breakfast. Take a quiet pill, give us all a rest from your yawping and righteous indignation, don't be getting all up in my grill, dog! I can assure you, other than what I write or sing about, I'm not getting up in yours and you can easily ignore me by just not buying my stuff or shunning any mention of me or my work you might ever see (and really, you won't see so much unless you come looking for me). Everybody just needs to calm down and go a little easier on those folks we love, but even easier on those we don't who may have voted for a different guy or girl than we did.

Get my meaning?

Thanks again for reading me here. I appreciate that all of our time is precious, I just hope, as I always do, that you, my reader, think your time was well spent reading my words.

My very best to you and yours.

PUBLISHER'S APPENDIX:
WRITING ISN'T JUST WORDS

Did you think we had finished this book? Did you look at the Table of Contents? Okay, no one usually looks at the Table of Contents.

As publisher, several elements made me want to produce this book. Ralph possesses an honesty that isn't discouraging, a writing voice that is both humorous and melodious without trying too hard (which connects back to his honesty, he's not pretending to be something/someone fancy), and his use of broad pop culture references.

Too often writers just mention other writers. Every author eventually writes a craft book. If you're a professional writer or if you have a BA in English acquired during the later half of the twentieth century, you probably know exactly what book I mean if I say, "Strunk & White."

There was a great social media post circulating that sounds like a joke. At least, it sounds like a joke if you work in any career associated with published words or have that English degree. A guy walks into the bookstore requesting a book for his daughter. He insists the title is "The Shrunken White Elephants of Style."

I laughed so hard I'm smiling even now. The bookstore employee finally realizes he means *The Elements of Style* by William Strunk Jr. and E.B. White. It's a classic. I have two copies. The one I bought back in my formative years and a second old copy someone gave me, because when you're the book nerd that's what people do, give you old books. As if my dust allergy needs that extra push.

So, yes, as writers, journalists, editors, authors, we *all* push certain books. Authors *love, love, love* Stephen King's *On Writing*. Ralph even references it. It's a good book. But let's face it, if Stephen King hadn't written it, no one would have opened it. But we *all* want to know how Stephen King became Stephen King. There are people who want to be Stephen King without even having read a Stephen King book.

And come on, after all those years of writing creepy horror fiction — my dog got hit by a car weeks after I read *Pet Sematary* as a teenager and I had nightmares he would come back from the grave as a demon dog — Stephen King got hit by a van while taking a leisurely walk and almost lost his leg. You need to show caution on how much weird you contribute to the universe. (That accident occurred June 19, 1999, and I remember wondering if Stephen King would die. Hard to believe that was almost 24 years ago to the day, as today is June 15.)

Other formidable titles include *On Writing Well* by William Zinsser, *Pity the Reader* by Kurt Vonnegut and Suzanne McConnell, *Fast Draft Your Memoir* by Rachael Herron, *Writing Down the Bones* by Natalie Goldberg, *Bird by Bird* by Anne Lamott, *The Writing Life* by Annie Dillard, *Write Your Novel from the Middle* by James Scott Bell... Need I go on? The only person not on the list is Dr. Seuss.

Though if he *did* write a book on craft, what would it sound like?

> I sit and I plot,
> I plot and I sit,
> I lift my pen
> and blot, blot, blot.
> First I write
> and then I type.
> I drink much coffee.
> It takes all night.

But in all seriousness, I have a point to all this literal nonsense. Books that discuss writing are great, and MFA programs that dissect writing have a place. In both cases, the book and the MFA program are useless if you are not doing the deed. Writing, that is. Just to be clear. This is a book about writing erotica. I don't want to mislead you on what deed. It's writing. That's why MFA programs spend *a lot* of time on writing and completing projects.

Parisian Phoenix Publishing highlights unique voices and diverse perspectives. That's what we wanted to do when we started, and it's how we approach every submission. First and foremost, we examine the voice and the perspective. The next step is to discuss the author's vision and how we can make a book that embodies the author's spirit. We call together the art director, the photographer and often a fine artist with the author.

In doing that, we realized how literary arts and visual arts need each other. Especially in today's world, where Midjourney and stock photos make "original" covers with custom-commissioned art a rarity. When the arts work together– that might be drawing, painting, photography, theatre, music, poetry, essays– then our brains fire on all cylinders. We unite the analytical and the creative mind.

And we unite as a community. None of us should stand alone.

So while *any* of the authors who wrote a book about craft can teach your rational mind something about grammar or plot, only a song or a movie or a finger painting or a certain way the sun flickers in the afternoon can spur the inspirational side of your brain in ways no book of rules ever would.

To take it even further, writers and editors who work with nonfiction have to follow rules. It's what keeps facts clear and sentences easy to interpret. Nonfiction's job is to teach you something, to make information you need to know stick in that crowded head of yours. But fiction — fuck the rules. Fiction dares you to follow a muse. Fiction double dares you to master those rules and then reach deep inside your subconscious and break them all like hooligan.

A purposeful, compelling hooligan.

That is why I asked Ralph to compile this big, ol' random list of his inspirations.

Maybe they will inspire you.

Or maybe you'll make your own list.

– Angel R. Ackerman

RALPH GRECO JR.'S INSPIRATION INDEX

ACTORS

Woody Allen. American comedian, actor, film director and writer. *Annie Hall, Manhattan, Match Point, Crimes and Misdemeanors* and many others have proved Allen's importance as one of the modern age's most prolific and interesting directors, in my opinion. Beginning his professional life in earnest as a writer for early American comedy shows, moving through a successful stand-up career then acting, writing and directing, Allen truly has no peers.

Alec Baldwin. American actor known for his roles in *Working Girl, The Hunt For Red October, Glengarry Glen Ross*, as mentioned above, and countless others. Might want to rethink trusting the guy with a handgun.

Sir Charles Spencer Chaplin, KBE. English born, but American icon. Writer, comedian, filmmaker, composer, reaching his highest level of popularity, stratospheric as it was, in the silent era of film. Charlie's full oeuvre is a must-see.

Frankie Russel Faison. An American actor known for roles like Commissioner Ervin Burrell of HBO's *The Wire* and Barney Matthews in the Hannibal Lecter franchise of films. As I note, he was also in one of my most favorite films of a more recent vintage, *Mother Night*, based on a Kurt Vonnegut novel of the same name.

Keith Gordon. Actor/director. In addition to directing the film version of *Mother Night*, he has directed countless television shows and other movies. His acting credits include *Jaws 2, All That Jazz, Dressed To Kill* and *Christine*.

Liam Neeson. I am referencing actor Liam Neeson here and his starring role in the 2008 movie *Taken*.

Oliver Platt. Canadian-born American actor. Appeared in many films, some of which include *Bulworth, Frost/Nixon, X-Men: First*

Class, countless television series, like *The West Wing*, *Nip/Tuck* and in Broadway plays like *Shining City*, and *Guys and Dolls*.

Pauly Montgomery Shore. Actor, comedian, filmmaker, writer. Known for his roles in *Encino Man*, *Bio- Dome* and *Son in Law*. He is the son of comedian Sammy Shore and Mitzi Shore. Mitzi was the owner and operator of the infamous L.A. nightclub the Comedy Store.

I recently caught a documentary of Shore that included some of his stand-up. It was pretty damn good stuff, actually. I know he is often counted out in the culture as a goofball, but one need be leery of how smart and funny Pauly Shore is.

Patrick Swayze. Actor, dancer, singer, known for starring in such films as *Dirty Dancing*, *Ghost* and *Road House*.

Robin McLaurin Williams was an actor and comedian, initially known for his wild improvisational style, early fame as "Mork," on the T.V. sitcom *Mork & Mindy*. He then went on to earn awards and nominations for many notable performances in films like *Good Will Hunting*, *Good Morning Vietnam*, *Dead Poets Society* and *The Fisher King*.

AUTHORS

Isaac Asimov. Considered one of the "Big Three" science fiction writers, with Robert A. Heinlein and Arthur C. Clarke (two more authors I would advise you to read), Asimov's astounding talent and prodigious output includes writing or editing over five hundred books, as well as penning ninety thousand letters and postcards. As well as writing the genre-breaking *Foundation*, *Robot* and *Galactic Empire* series, Asimov also wrote countless mysteries and non-fiction.

Another biggie writer in my world…and really, what else matters other than what happens in my world?

François-Marie Arouet. Known by his nom de plume M. de Voltaire was a French writer of plays, poems, fiction, essays, writing over 20k letters and 2k books and pamphlets. As an outspoken advocate for civil liberties and the separation of church and state, he came under consistent strict censor attempts by the Catholic French monarchy. His best-known work is the novella *Candide*.

Ray Douglas Bradbury-Where do I begin about my most favorite writer? I've never understood why Bradbury is not considered among the aforementioned Big Three (ok, he would be the fourth) seeing as, for me, Bradbury is just as important as pretty much any author, science fiction writer or anybody else. Bradbury would never have called himself a science fiction writer, though.

Bradbury wrote so much across so many different genres, from his seminal themed science fiction short story collection *The Martian Chronicles* to screenplays and T.V. scripts, like his screenplay for John Houston's *Moby Dick* to the gut-wrenching, best short story I have ever read "The Laurel and Hardy Love Affair," the man's pure poetry word-flow hurts to read at times, he is just that good.

M. Christian. Although his Wikipedia page lists my friend as an author and anthologist (but not anthropologist) who has crossed many genres with his work (among them horror, futurism, science fiction and erotica), I could never explain how much my buddy has influenced my writing life and professional kink convention romping, provided fodder for countless in-person, on-the-phone, and across-our-podcast geek-out laughfests. But I'll keep it professional and stop my gushing.

"Chris," as he is known to his friends (and pretty much everybody who meets the guy regards him as a friend) is the kind of writer I would love to be one day. A mentor, friend and partner-in-crime (although nothing ever happened on U.S. soil so we are safe) as I advise too often in this book, really, ***this is a guy you have to go out and read if you have not done so.*** Delving into a short, short story by M. Christian or a 70-word column will make your life better in ways I could never rightly describe.

Roald Dahl. British author of books, short stories and poetry, best known for penning classic children's titles such as, *James and the Giant Peach, Matilda*, and *Charlie and the Chocolate Factory*, from which one of my most favorite films, *Willy Wonka and the Chocolate Factory* (the Gene Wilder original, thank you very much) is based.

Joan Didion. Premier American writer of essay and fiction. Contemporaries include writers such as Gay Talese and Tom Wolfe, all part of what has been called "New Journalism" style. The literary technique Didion and her fellows perfected center around a highly subjective view infecting what has normally been thought of as long-form non-fiction writing. I just think she is a fantastically great essayist.

Harlan Jay Ellison. Writer Ellison is regarded as one of the leading authors of modern speculative fiction, essays, teleplays and screenplays, and just about anything else he took his pen and opinion to. Highly prolific, considered by many as much a talented writer as an opinionated enfant terrible (one of the reasons I love the guy so much). In his lifetime, Ellison wrote nearly two-thousand short stories, countless screenplays, comic scripts, essays and criticism. I consider Ellison in the same illustrious company as favorites of mine like Mark Twain, Robert Sheckley, and Kurt Vonnegut and any other writer of note you could name.

Ian Fleming. British author and creator of James Bond.

Neil Richard MacKonnin Gaiman. An English writer of short stories, novels, comics, graphic novels, audio works and screenwriter. His infamous *The Sandman* comic series and novels *American Gods* and *The Ocean at the End of the Lane* have thrust him foremost in high regard of fantastic modern fiction.

Ralph Greco Jr. I just wanted to see my name listed with Gaiman.

Winston Groom. Author of the novel that preceded the Oscar award-winning movie, **Forrest Gump**. See Movies.

Ernest Miller Hemingway. Leading American novelist, short-story writer, and journalist. Known for his lean prose style.

Christopher Eric Hitchens. British-born author and journalist, and as he called himself, a celebrated "anti-theist," Hitchens was a writer, lecturer and quite often T.V. talk show guest. Hitchen's many published works include critical biographies of Mother Teresa and Bill Clinton, pieces for various magazines, and one of my personal favorites of his 2007 *God Is Not Great*. Agree with him or not (and I did both) Hitchens was one of those big brain contrarians I feel we need more of these days.

E.L. (Erika Mitchell) James. Author of the wildly popular *Fifty Shades of Grey, Fifty Shades Darker* and *Fifty Shades Freed* trilogy of modern BDSM literature. Derided among the self-appointed erotic literati as "mommy porn," meaning women at home raising kids were mostly the ones enjoying/getting off on E.L. James' books, the criticism is subjective at best, as criticism always is. Any writer in the world salivates when reading that E.L.'s books have sold over one-hundred-and-fifty million copies worldwide, with thirty-five million of them in the US alone.

Good for her, I say.

Stephen King. Popular American novelist. All but reinventing modern horror in book form, his prolific output, from *Carrie, Salem's Lot,* to *The Shining* and *It* and many, many more has earned him sales of over for hundred million copies and seen his novels made into feature films, comic books and television series. I happen to think his *On Writing: A Memoir of the Craft* is one of the best books about writing.

Ursula K. Le Guin. Celebrated speculative fiction writer. Her *Earthsea Trilogy* pretty much consumed my life for a good year. As it was when I read *The Lord Of The Rings* by J.R.R. Tolkien my junior year of high school, I became mired in this trilogy, having to cleanse my palate between each book course by reading a few others totally unrelated to the trilogy I was presently slogging through. This was why it usually took me a good year to read through these long series (C.S. Lewis' *Narnia Chronicles* being another). For me it was like sitting down at a multicourse meal and making it last as long as I could.

"Papa." nickname **Ernest Hemingway** was known by.

Edgar Allan Poe. A writer I find particularly difficult to describe given how much I love him. Poe was an American writer, editor and literary critic, his famous poem "The Raven," setting the standard for gothic imagery in the form like no other and short stories such a "The Tell-

Tale Heart," "The Fall of the House of Usher," and "The Masque of the Red Death," taking on horror conventions like none before, or quite frankly since. And extraordinarily campy as they are, and loosely based on his work, I am not above referring you to the AIP (American International Pictures) produced series of horror films inspired by Poe's stories and poetry. These were staples of the 4:30 Movie when I was a kid that my friends and I lovingly devoured every time they played. In their way, I believe these 1960-era films prompted a generation to go searching for Poe's written works.

Regarded as one of the true innovators of the modern short story form, Poe is also credited with creating the modern detective genre in publishing his infamous "The Murders in the Rue Morgue" story.

Anne Rampling, see **Anne Rice**.

Anne Rice. American author of gothic novels, including her infamous *The Vampire Chronicles*, plus erotica, written under the names Anne Rampling and A. N. Roquelaure. There was a time when all I did was read Rice.

A. N. Roquelaure, see **Anne Rice.**

Willy S.: William Shakespeare.

Aaron Benjamin Sorkin. American playwright, screenwriter and film director, Sorkin's work includes writing and creating the television series, *The West Wing* and *The Newsroom* (to name just two), playwriting *A Few Good Men* and *The Farnsworth Invention,* and penning the screenplays for *The American President, Moneyball* and *Molly's Game*… again, to name just a few.

Gertrude Stein. Novelist/poet/playwright/art collector. While born in America, Stein famously moved to Paris in 1903, where she hosted a "salon" (in this context the word is simply a fancy-shmancy way of saying a great big old hang of like-minded creatives) welcoming leading artists from the literature and art worlds.

Jean Marie Stine. A luminary in the world of letters, award-winning writer, publisher, editor, anthologist, Jean Marie worked through the fantastic fiction field in the 1960's and 1970's, has penned countless pieces of fiction and non-fiction and wrote what is considered a seminal work of transgender science fiction, *Season of the Witch*.

I met Jean Marie when I met Chris, in San Francisco in 2009 and she was the first publisher to release a full book of my erotica. A luminary in many genres of writing, one of the earliest people to publish erotica online, I consider her a very good friend and my go-to publisher.

Lee Strasberg- American theatre director, actor and acting teacher, director of NYC's Actor's Studio and later its L.A. counterpart.

Jonathan Swift. All of us stand on the shoulders of giants and for writers and lovers of satire, there are none bigger and broader than old Jonathan Swift's. As the author of such classics as *Gulliver's Travels*, and "A Modest Proposal," to name but a few, the term "Swiftian" became nearly synonymous with the word satire. For me, the greatest satirist of all time.

Dylan Marlais Thomas. Welsh poet and writer, whose famous poem "Do not go gentle into that good night," alone pretty much secures the man legendary literature status. Absolutely impossible to classify his poetry as from any one school or imbuing any particular style (much to his delight it seems) Thomas is considered a primary man of letters of the past century.

Mark Twain. Author, essayist, lecturer, renown American literary luminary. Another huge influence on me. *The Adventures of Huckleberry Finn*, *Pudd'nhead Wilson*, *The Adventures of Tom Sawyer* are just a few of the classics he wrote. Interestingly, as he grew older, Twain became as well-known as a lecturer as he was an author, which is kind of how I see my career spinning in these later years now…if I could ever get anybody to sit and listen to me yap or I truly had something interesting to say.

Kurt Vonnegut. Along with Bradbury, Poe, and Ellison, I'd have to say that Kurt Vonnegut has been one of the biggest influences on my reading and writing. One of the true modern-day satirists, working within the fantasist genre mostly, like Robert Sheckley (another big influence on me) Vonnegut's darkly humorous novels (he published forty in his lifetime) essays, plays, and short stories set the man in a league of his own. Vonnegut's *Slaughterhouse-Five* is a classic satirical anti-war exploration and brought him his first big fame, fortune and to the lecture circuit, where I was lucky to have seen him.

Voltaire, see **François-Marie Arouet.**

Alice Walker. American writer of novels, short stories, poetry, Walker holds the distinction of being the first African-American woman to win the Pulitzer Prize for fiction, for her book *The Color Purple,* see more in books.

Roger Joseph Zelazny. I have to thank my buddy Bob for turning me on to this amazing writer. Zelazny wrote a score of short stories and novels in his lifetime, but is best known for *The Chronicles of Amber* series (again, as I advise all throughout this book, something you damn well need to read...right now!)

BOOKS

1984. I can't even begin to explain how George Orwell's *1984* messed me up for weeks when I read it junior year of high school. I was one of those people who always had a book in his hand, something I was reading beyond anything I was ever assigned in school and round about the age of sixteen I got into the classic lot of dystopian novels: Yevgeny Zamyatin's *We*, Aldous Huxley's *Brave New World* and Orwell's *1984*. One could even include Ray Bradbury's *Fahrenheit 451* into this mix, though there is infinitely more hope in Bradbury's classic novel than in any of these other three.

Actually, I was a very happy teen, my reading material notwithstanding.

Amber Chronicles. Also known as *The Chronicles of Amber.* This is author Roger Joseph Zelazny's most famous work...and for a reason. Are you still here? Didn't I tell you above to go read these books? Jesus, what the hell are you waiting for?!

"Beauty" series. A four-book series written by Anne Rice working under the pen name A. N. Roquelaure. These stories concern the character Beauty and her adventures in a mythical kinkdom (yes, that misspelling is intentional) and the punishments/delights she is subjected to. To paraphrase Jerry Lee Lewis, in these books there's a "whole lotta spankin' goin' on." For a time, these were the books that my friends and I devoured, but as with anything, too much of even kinky sex can wear thin after a while. Best read one at a time, with lots of other books in-between.

Belinda. 1986 Anne Rice novel she wrote under the pseudonym, Anne Rambling. My story about this one, if you want to hear it (well, you have no choice, unless you just skip past this) is that I gave this erotic mystery to a friend of mine just before she left on her honeymoon. When she returned with her new hubby, the man joked-complained that the entire time he was away with my friend he could hardly get her nose out of *Belinda*.

Candide. Original name *Candide, ou l'Optimisme*, French satire written by Voltaire. When I was introduced to this my freshman year in college I was set on my way to explore and try to write satire.

The Color Purple. Seminal novel by Alice Walker, published in 1982 and winning the Pulitzer Prize a year later. Later adapted into a movie and musical.

Charlie and the Chocolate Factory. Roald Dahl book published in 1964, centered around Charlie Bucket's adventures inside the chocolate factory of Willy Wonka.

Fifty Shades of Grey. The first novel in E.L. James trilogy, featuring the characters of dominant Christian Grey and budding submissive Anastasia Steele. See Authors.

Little Women. Classic American coming-of-age novel written by American novelist Louisa May Alcott.

The Martian Chronicles. Called a 'fix-up' novel, meaning the book consists of previously-published short stories, connected by short 'bridges' of narratives, Ray Bradbury's famous science-fiction book was published in 1950. It deals with humans leaving Earth after a nuclear war, settling Mars as well as the drama that ensues when the Martians are beset by their colonizers.

A Moveable Feast. A memoir written by Ernest Hemingway concerning his years as a writer living in Paris in the 1920's. The book was published posthumously in 1964.

Mother Night. 1961 novel written by Kurt Vonnegut.

On Writing: A Memoir of the Craft. Written by Stephen King and published in 2000, this is a wonderful book on writing, the second of two I'd recommend on the craft, (I'm way too humble to recommend the book you are presently reading to put mine in the same company), the other being Ray Bradbury's *Zen in the Art of Writing: Essays on Creativity.*

Twilight. The first book of author Stephenie Meyer's romantic fantasy book series, featuring teen vampires and werewolves locked in battles over their lusts, angst and just about whatever else teens, supernatural and not, get into.

The Witching Hour. Anne Rice novel published in 1990. Beginning the trilogy, that includes *Lasher* and *Taltos.* The basis for the most recent AMC television series *Mayfair Witches,* this book saw me through some very tough times in my early 30s, as books often do help us with life.

MAGAZINES AND OTHER PUBLICATIONS

New Yorker, The. Another big-time fiction market that's nearly impossible to crack. First published in 1925, this stalwart of American writing is considered one of the top American magazines (and a weekly at that) publishing satire, cartoons, essays, criticism and fiction. Yes, another mag I can brag constant rejection from.

Paris Review, The. A quarterly literary magazine begun in the city it is named after in the early 1950's. Heavy duty, non-genre writers like Philip Roth, Samuel Beckett, Jack Kerouac have been published here. The magazine moved its offices to New York city in 1973 and was edited by George Plimpton, arguably during its most high-publicized era. It continues today in that city and routinely rejects me.

Penthouse Letters. A seemingly 'letters'-led glossy publication released from the Penthouse corporation. My first professional erotic fiction sales were made to this magazine. They published two of my stories, for what was at that time (and kinda still is) a whopping $350.00.

Zines. Short for "fanzine," are small-circulation, self-published, compilations of text, pictures and illustrations, or all three (pretty much anything someone wants to put on a page) created by an organization or group to either espouse that groups' ethos, a collective's interest or output from members.

MOVIES

Field Of Dreams. A 1989 American sports fantasy film written and directed by Phil Alden, starring Kevin Costner and James Earl Jones, based on W.P. Kinsella's 1982 novel, *Shoeless Joe*. Like Forrest Gump, there are some iconic scenes as well as dialogue uttered in this movie, one of which is the famous "If you build it, they will come."

Forrest Gump. This 1994 movie, based on a novel by Winston Groom, starred Tom Hanks, Robin Wright and Gary Sinise. It is as much a melodrama I feel as a soft-ball satire. There are several notable quotes that have been lifted from the film to become popular in modern day lexicon, one of the most famous being, "Mama always said life was like a box of chocolates. You never know what you're gonna get."

To which I always add, "Well, at the very least, you're sure to get chocolate."

After the success of the film, Groom released a Forrest Gump sequel in 1995.

Glengarry Glen Ross 1992 American film written by David Mamet, from his 1984 Pulitzer Prize-winning play of the same name. Brutal indictment of corporate sales, starring Alan Arkin, Ed Harris, Jack Lemon, Al Pacino and Alex Baldwin.

The Godfather. Another favorite of mine that's hard to rightly describe as I pretty much have to get up off my knees as I genuflect to any mention made of this 1972 movie. Directed by Francis Ford Coppola, based on Mario Puzo's novel of the same name and starring Marlon Brando, James Caan, Al Pacino and too many more unbelievable actors to name, here is another movie replete with fantastic quotes, scenes and pretty much non-stop movie-making gold. There is also the cinematography of Gordon Willis to salivate over.

The Godfather, Part II-Film that followed the 1972 film *The Godfather*, directed once again by Francis Ford Coppola, partly based on Mario Puzo's original *The Godfather* novel. The movie unfolds quite uniquely as both a prequel to *The Godfather* and a sequel and is another movie that I simply love.

The Hannibal Lecter Franchise. Mentioned above, these four movies are based around the fictional serial killer, Hannibal Lecter, created by Thomas Harris and appearing in his books *Red Dragon, The Silence of the Lambs, Hannibal,* and *Hannibal Rising*. Anthony Hopkins played the flesh-eating Doctor Lecter in three of these films and won an Academy Award for his portrayal of him in the film version of, *The Silence Of The Lambs*.

Roadhouse. 1989 American action film, starring Patrick Swayze, Sam Elliot, Kelly Lynch and Ben Gazzara.

Springsteen on Broadway. Netflix documentary on New Jersey rocker, Bruce Springsteen.

MUSIC

A&R men. The abbreviation stands for "artist and repertoire." This was (and it was more than is these days in the music business) the division of a record label or music publishing company responsible for courting and signing talent and overseeing that talent's development.

Beauty And The Beast. The last song on Stevie Nicks' 1983 solo album *The Wild Heart*

The Boss. Nickname given to Bruce Springsteen.

Don't Stop Believin'. Rock band Journey had a massive hit with this song in 1981. "Don't Stop Believin'" written by the band's vocalist Steve Perry, guitarist Neal Schon and keyboardist Jonathan Cain has become the best-selling digital track of the 20th century. (It was also the soundtrack for the Atari 2600 video game "Journey Escape" where gamers had to get members of the band to the tour bus avoiding barricades, fans and other obstacles.)

Emerson, Lake and Palmer. Seminal 1970s "progressive-rock" trio from the UK. Consisting of keyboardist, songwriter Keith Emerson, vocalist/guitarist/songwriter/producer Greg Lake and drummer/percussionist/songwriter Carl Palmer. ELP is my personal holy trinity when it comes to music; for me, there is none better. I could go on and on about how ELP, Yes, Pink Floyd, Jethro Tull, Supertramp, all these vintage/classic rock bands made my life what it is, but I shan't bore you. Go seek out some Youtube videos of these bands if you have never heard of them…then prepare to have your DNA alerted.

Roberta Cleopatra Flack. American singer who topped the early 1970s music charts with the No. 1 singles "The First Time Ever I Saw Your Face" and the song I am referencing "Killing Me Softly with His Song."

Norman Jeffrey "Jeff" Healey. Blind Canadian guitarist who played across many styles. Most known for playing electric guitar on his lap.

Journey. American rock band formed in San Francisco in 1973. Their monstrous MTV-era run of hits, "Don't Stop Believin'" "Open Arms," "Separate Ways (Worlds Apart)" and "Faithfully," (to name but a few) are FM staples to this day. But I refer you to the band pre-Steve Perry joining and even the first album Perry appears on, *Infinity*, to get the full range of what this band was like prior to their explosive popularity.

You might be pleasantly surprised.

Mick. I mean Mick Jagger here, lead singer, songwriter and harmonica player (the instrument his fellow bandmate, guitarist and co-songwriter Keith Richards says Mick plays exceptionally well) sings and co-wrote The Rolling Stones hit "Jumpin' Jack Flash," which contains a repeated lyric of "gas, gas, gas."

Stevie Nicks. Singer, songwriter. Most famously known as a member of rock band Fleetwood Mac, Nicks has gone on to score countless hit singles and albums during a solo career that is still alive and well.

Southside Johnny. Singer/songwriter John Lyon uses the stage name "Southside Johnny," fronting his American band *Southside Johnny and the Asbury Jukes*.

The Wild Heart. Solo album by Stevie Nicks of Fleetwood Mac.

NOTABLE PEOPLE

Jeffrey Preston Bezos. American entrepreneur, best known as the founder and executive chairman of Amazon.

James Bond. Famous fictional spy made famous in Ian Fleming's books and countless movies made across many decades. Also known as 007. And just for the record, since I know you are keeping track of these things, Sean Connery will always be the only Bond for me.

Chim-Chim. Cartoon chimpanzee character from Speed Racer cartoon.

Anne Frank. German-born Jewish girl who hid out in a secret section of an apartment with her family in Nazi's occupied Amsterdam during World War 11. Her diary, *The Diary of a Young Girl*, usually referred to as "The Diary of Anne Frank," published posthumously in 1947 is a celebrated non-fiction work on the Holocaust and considered of the modern world's most important books.

Judge Judith Sheindlin. A U.S. courtroom reality show star who presides over a mock courtroom built for her *Judge Judy* television program.

Cesar Milan (César Felipe Millán Favela). Mexican-American dog trainer, TV personality, known as the "Dog Whisperer."

J.F.K. John Fitzgerald Kennedy, 35th President of the United States.

Jo March. One of the March sisters. Character in Louisa May Alcott's novel, *Little Women*.

Friedrich Gustav Emil Martin Niemöller. German theologian and Lutheran pastor best known for his famous 1946 poem "First they came…" In full the quote reads: "First they came for the socialists, and I did not speak out — because I was not a socialist. Then they came for the trade unionists, and I did not speak out — because I was not a trade unionist. Then they came for the Jews, and I did not speak out — because I was not a Jew. Then they came for me — and there was no one left to speak for me."

Dr. Jordan Bernt Peterson. Canadian psychologist, author, Youtube star, lecturer. Peterson has gained widespread attention the past decade and half for his views on everything from transgenderism to politics. He came to my attention over his country's attempt to enact compelled speech legislation into law.

To me, as non-political a person you are ever likely to find, still, a government compelling speech is some pretty serious shit!

Ron Popeil. Founded the company Ronco in the early 60s and his kitschy inexpensive inventions, mostly kitchen items, became ubiquitous across the American landscape. Popeil's personal informercials — he might indeed be the inventor of this way of TV selling — became even more famous then his inventions like The Pocket Fisherman, Inside-the-Shell Egg Scrambler and his many "-O-Matic" products like The Chop-O-Matic, the Veg-O-Matic and the Dial-O-Matic. The Veg-O-Matic actually sits in Washington D.C.'s Smithsonian museum.

Hyman Roth. Character played by Lee Strasberg in *The Godfather, Part 11*.

President Donald Trump. NYC-based business man and 45th President of the United States.

Henry "Henny" Youngman. British-born American comedian, known for taking the stage with a violin, he hardly, if ever played, delivered short jokes in such rapid fashion he became known as "the King of the One-Liners." His famous being "Take my wife…please!"

PLACES

Waldorf Astoria Hotel. Luxury hotel/residence, built in the Art Deco style, sitting between 49th and 50th street on Park Ave. in New York City.

The River Styx. From Greek mythology, goddess and river of the Underworld.

PLAY

Shining City. Conor McPherson wrote this play based around a ghost story where a widower regales his therapist with the story of seeing his dead wife. I caught Oliver Platt starring on Broadway in this show, which he earned a "Best Actor" Tony Award for.

QUOTES

"A Rose is a Rose is a Rose." From the poem "Sacred Emily" by Gertrude Stein that contains the infamous line "Rose is a rose is a rose is a rose" often shortened to "A rose is a rose is a rose" and usually interpreted as meaning things are as simple as what they are. The scuttlebutt I heard in college (the few times I was actually paying attention in one of my English Major undergraduate courses and not just chasing girls… oh boy where these the daze!) was that G.S. was as much making a statement on the law of identity as she was giving Shakespeare a little nudge in the ribs over his "A rose by any other name would smell as sweet," line from *Romeo and Juliet*, and other references to a rose in literature before and even her time meant so much more than simply the flower.

Catch-22. Phrase coined from the famous 1961 Joseph Heller novel of the same name. Interestingly enough, the number here was picked arbitrarily, as supposedly one of Heller's publishers, born on the 22nd of October thought 22 was funnier than 18, the original number Heller was going to use in the title. In modern usage, a Catch-22 describes a paradox from which a person cannot soon escape given its conflicting, often ironic conditions.

"First they came…" poem by Friedrich Gustav Emil Martin Niemöller. In full the quote reads: "First they came for the socialists, and I did not speak out — because I was not a socialist. Then they came for the trade unionists, and I did not speak out — because I was not a trade unionist. Then they came for the Jews, and I did not speak out — because I was not a Jew. Then they came for me — and there was no one left to speak for me."

"Gas, gas, gas." Repeated lyric within The Rolling Stones' hit "Jumpin' Jack Flash."

"If you build it, they will come." See movies, **Field of Dreams.**

Pudd'nhead's basket warning. The famous quote from Mark Twain's 1894 novel *Pudd'nhead Wilson* is "Pull all your eggs in the one basket and — WATCH THAT BASKET."

"We choose to go to the Moon" speech. JFK speech, officially titled the "Address at Rice University on the Nation's Space Effort," delivered on September 12th, 1962 to bolster support for the U.S. space exploration effort and JFK's proposal to land a man on the Moon before the end of the decade.

SEXUALITY TERMS

BDSM. Abbreviation for erotic power-play sexual pursuits involving bondage dominance, submission and/or sadomasochism. These days the term is used as an umbrella description for all kinds of non-vanilla sexual interests.

Chastity. Although the Oxford dictionary defines chastity as the "practice of refraining from extramarital, or especially from all, sexual intercourse," in the context that I am using it, I mean the BDSM (see above) practice of denying your sub/partner/lover/friend-with-benees sexual release.

Pegging. Ok, here we get into some naughty stuff (it's about time). This is the sexual act where one partner penetrates the other's anus, usually with a strap-on dildo.

Pyrex dildos. Sex toys made from hard glass-like material. While not so very malleable, Pyrex can be heated and cooled to add extra sensations to how a dildo usually feels. Wowza!

TELEVISION

Matlock. American broadcast T.V. mystery show starring actor Andy Griffith in the title role of criminal defense attorney Ben Matlock. Aired from 1986–1992, then again from 1992–1995.

The Outer Limits. As with *Star Trek*, and most things I reference in this book, I mean the original television series that ran on American television from September 1963 to January 1965. Employing writers like Harlan Ellison, Joseph Stefano (writer of Hitchcock's film *Psycho*) and future *Chinatown* screenwriter Robert Towne and many more notables, the self-contained hour episodes are considered, along with the show's contemporary *The Twilight Zone*, to have aired some of the very best science fiction and speculative programming ever.

Let me tell you a little story about how erotic writing brought me into a one-degree of separation encounter with the original *The Outer Limits* series ("Oh no, Ralph, even here in the footnotes you have to regale us with a story?!" I hear you cry). This is a good one, I promise, and it even includes M. Christian, and even some connection to kink.

Chris and I were in St. Louis the second year in a row to teach at a kink convention that we had once again been flown out to. This is about the best it gets for guys like us attending these conventions. Our flights, rooms and meals all 'comped' by the convention's organizers, with Chris and I not seeing one another all that often (he lives in Ore., me in N.J.) we relish the hang even over then teaching a class or visiting a city rife with kinksters.

As this was our second time out that way, we hooked-up once again with the convention's driver, a great guy named Rosie, who Chris and I just came to adore. Knowing the city as well as he did, Rosie told us of a great late-night diner he often went to, and Chris and I, being fans of cool out-of-the-way local spots, went out on Saturday night driven by Rosie, while the convention was in full dungeon swing (and I do mean 'swing') to eat at this spot. Sitting down in the booth, we all began to tell of our life and Chris and I found out that Rosie, a good ten years older than Chris and I, had lived in L.A. in the 1960's. And he had worked with the company that made all the masks and costume creature apparatus for the old *Outer Limits* show.

You can bet Chris and I were salivating over more than just the delicious and plentiful food as Rosie regaled us and we ate it all up like the fanboys we are.

Ronco. Ron Popeil founded the company Ronco in the early 60s and his kitschy inexpensive inventions, mostly kitchen items, became ubiquitous across the American landscape. Popeil's personal informercials — he might indeed be the inventor of this way of TV selling — became even more famous then his inventions like The Pocket Fisherman, Inside-the-Shell Egg Scrambler and his many "-O-Matic" products like The Chop-O-Matic, the Veg-O-Matic and the Dial-O-Matic. The Veg-O-Matic actually sits in Washington D.C.'s Smithsonian museum.

Scooby-Doo. American Saturday morning animated television series *Scooby-Doo, Where Are You!* launched in 1969. The title character is a dog.

Seinfeld. American television sitcom created by Larry David and Jerry Seinfeld, that ran from July 5, 1989, to May 14, 1998.

Star Trek. There are just those influences I can't extricate myself from, nor do I want to. The original *Star Trek* T.V. series, running from 1966-1969, created by Gene Roddenberry and starring Willian Shatner, Leonard Nimoy and DeForest Kelley is my all-time most favorite television show, and something I reference consistently in my life and writing. All other *Star Trek* series and the series' many movies, do not even rate on the old radar as far as I am concerned when set against this first (and best) trip of men (and women) boldly going "where no man has gone before."

I first set my eyes on the OG Trek when it was repeated in the early 1970's, too young to really understand it all that much on its first run. Besotted by it from first blush, I often brag that the first-ever science-fiction convention I ever attended, was the second Star Trek convention, held in New York city in 1973, famously overrun by fans. This is when William Shatner, yes Captain Kirk himself, talked to me personally… making an announcement to a group of us standing up on a table mid-center of a large hotel ballroom to sit down so those behind us could see.

Yes, a brush with greatness for little twelve-year-old me!

Ted Lasso. Apple TV sports comedy drama series.

VOCABULARY

AI (artificial intelligence) programs. Computer intelligence that has learned from the vast material on the internet to interact with humans, perform research, and create responses. The most famous of which in 2023, is ChatGPT, developed by the company OpenAI, released in November of 2022. This tech is being used and considered from its seemingly limitless versatility to create non-fiction, fiction and sound recordings; basically anything and everything we humans can make. Yes, Cybernet is here.

A.P. (Associated Press) Style. A constant thorn in my side when it comes to writing press releases or pretty much any non-fiction writing that I know has the potential to be disseminated by the masses. This 'style' of writing (more like Draconian rules that seemingly change at whim) is used to provide what is deemed 'consistent' (and therein lies the rub; 'consistent,' I laugh at the word!) grammar, spelling and overall language usage, by newspapers, magazines and PR departments across the U.S.

Oh, don't get me started…

Author's copy. Copy of the author's book usually provided by the publisher to the author free of charge.

Computer Dictation Programs. If you are familiar with the Star Trek conceit, first introduced in the original (and only as far as I'm concerned

Star Trek) of cast members talking to computers to glean answers and enact commands, then you already have a good understanding of what a computer dictation program is. In this case, the program types the words a speaker utters into a document either on a desktop screen or a mobile device.

Craig's List. An online site for classified advertisements that include job listings, forums and sale items.

Dopamine. Neurotransmitter chemical released by nerve cells to send signals to other nerve cells. I use it in the text to describe how dopamine affects the 'firing' of the pleasure centers of the brain.

Double-dipping. Made popular on the Seinfeld sitcom, when a character dipped a chip into a dip, took a bite of that chip, then dipped it back into the dip.

Ghostwriting. Writing where someone else writes in the style or 'voice' of another person, who puts their name to the work. Something I have done often in my writing career.

Google Docs. Word processing program offered free to Google users. Available as a mobile app and desktop application.

Grammarly. Online grammar check program that has been in use since 2009, and like GPS, and many other social media apps, is slowly robbing us of the ability to think.

Again, I say, don't get me started.

Kevas and Trillium. Fictional substances created in the original *Star Trek* television series.

Moral Turpitude. Legal concept referring to any action or behavior that runs contrary to the community standards of honesty, justice, and upstanding virtue. Yes, you can see where many of us, not just smut writers, but a whole bunch of folks, could get ensnared in the definitions and judgments here.

Naturopath. A practitioner of healing through preventative measures such as diet, exercise, massage, etc.

Neo-Luddite. Philosophy opposing many forms of modern technology. Based on the historical legacy of the English Luddites, active between 1811 and 1816.

Onomatopoeia. Words imitating the sound referenced: "buzz" and "boom," Edgar Allen Poe demonstrated this in "The Bells," a four-part poem published posthumously in 1849.

Orwellian. Referring to George Orwell and the state-led oppression and spying featured in his bleak masterpiece, *1984*.

Rickard Olla. My made-up slang, meaning nothing at all or "dick olla."

Romulan. Alien face (alien to humans that is) enemy to *Star Trek* crew and Federation, debuting in the first *Star Trek* series. At one point the Romulans developed a clocking device that rendered their ship invisible. Don't worry, Captain Kirk went over and stole it in "The Enterprise Incident" episode.

Series runner. Also known as a Showrunner, this is a top executive producer of a television production. Sometimes, not always, this person is the creator of the show.

Sisyphean task. According to Greek mythology, Sisyphus was a king who annoyed the gods so much they set him to an eternity's punishment of rolling a big rock up a steep hill in the underworld only to watch it roll back down every time. A Sisyphean task is an endeavor that's generally regarded as unending.

Talamasca. Also known as the Order of the Talamasca, is a fictional secret society of paranormal researchers created by Anne Rice and appearing in both her *The Vampire Chronicles* and *Lives of the Mayfair Witches* series.

Whac-A-Mole. An arcade game where the plastic heads of 'moles' pop from a waist-level surface 'play area' while the player attempts to bash these heads with a large mallet. Fun for the whole family.

The Fashion and Fiends Series
By Angel Ackerman

Manipulations | Courting Apparitions | Recovery

Angel Ackerman's *Fashion and Fiends* series blends the suspense and fear of contemporary horror fiction with the humor and lightheartedness of late twentieth-century "chick lit." Her diverse network of characters experience the richness and depth of human struggle, which is why while the characters in the universe fall in love and pursue their happily-ever-after, the series can't quite be called paranormal romance.

Ackerman uses magic and the supernatural to explore weighted topics like domestic violence, body image and self-esteem, depression and grief, colonialism, women's rights, coming-of-age, religion, infibulation, infertility, and blended families. As Ackerman's characters navigate their world, they share the same plights their readers do.

Purchase these titles and more at your favorite independent bookseller or online retailer including Bookshop.org.

The saga continues—"Road Trip"—available Christmas, 2023.

DO YOU WANT TO HELP PARISIAN PHOENIX OR ANY SMALL PUBLISHER OR INDEPENDENT AUTHOR?

- Buy books. Buy more books. Give books as gifts.
- Recommend authors to friends.
- Share Social Media Posts.
- Leave a review:

  Amazon

  Goodreads

  Google Books

  Learn how 🢂

  - ○ Readers use reviews to find books.
  - ○ Retailers' web sites use reviews as part of their algorithm.
  - ○ Some advertisers require a certain number of reviews.
- Join and share newsletters.
- Attend events.
- Join Goodreads and follow authors, mark their books as read, shelve and rate them.
- Check on Patreon and Kickstarter for the creators you love
- Start a book club.

Subscribe to our Newsletter, "Bookish Babble", on

https://parisianphoenixpublishing.substack.com/

www.ingramcontent.com/pod-product-compliance
Lightning Source LLC
Chambersburg PA
CBHW071154120626
46546CB00006B/2257